Woodworking for Kids

The Ultimate Guide to Introduce Kids to Woodworking.

• Over 80 Easy Step-by-Step Projects with Images for Children. •

LESS WOOD
PUBLISHING

★ *Less Wood Publishing* ★

Table of Contents

Introduction

Following pioneering work by Friedrich Froebel, kindergarten movement founder, the earliest records of woodworking in early childhood education emerged. His children's view was as integrated learners who studied with their minds and minds more efficiently through becoming involved. Froebel stressed allowing children constructive participation in realistic thinking, and while pursuing passions, he believed in incorporating creativity with physical activity.

There is no convincing proof that under his kindergarten arrangement, Froebel himself was specifically supplying woodwork, but it was soon accepted as an extra profession when Froebel's kindergarten concepts spread across the globe. In his former school in Keilhau, Froebel initiated woodwork for older children and included them in several major building ventures at the farm. At the Froebel's original kindergarten time in Blankenburg, perhaps it would have been complex for young children to manage the tools that were then available, as only available were large tools.

It seems Froebel himself had a natural connection to timber. Maybe the growing up experience in eastern Germany's rural countryside, living in wooden built a beautiful house and childhood much spending playing in the large wooden attic or the woods, all had an impact. The teachings of Froebel emphasized playing and learning via natural materials connection and nature experiences seen by him as both souls nurturing and vital for the holistic development of the children.

Gifts

Initially, Froebel introduced wooden children gifts: tangible objects three-dimensional sets that could increase curiosity and be manipulated, exploration encouraging, connecting, and, in particular, developing spatial thought.

Occupations

Then, Froebel introduced 'Occupations,' which expanded on gifts, providing greater materials diversity, and greater exploration opportunities. This work shows the developing skills of life and was partly seen as preparing for manual training later and also the future work allowing kids to experience reconstructing through play and move from solid to the more abstract thought. Working with paper, sewing, parquetry, painting, weaving, wood, and clay were included in occupations somewhere between 1860-1880. Wood became part of the Occupations group, which included the solid forms – that also included clay work and build kits. Not included although the occupations set in the beginning, very popular became woodwork addition dating later back to around 1860. In Keilhau a school had co-founded by Froebel before inventing his kindergarten. The original workshop is present still in this school and to this very day, it continues to support woodwork. Older children have been involved very much in the school actual construction and for many years the children have been working on woodworking projects in large numbers like in the woods, building some cabin.

Very carefully the materials were selected to help in developing the child's 2-and-3-dimensional form understanding, develop skills of problem-solving, physical development support, representing and communicating ideas for creative expression. Froebel hoped they would acquire a greater connection understanding of life and nature generally by connecting with these carefully chosen natural materials. The Occupations truly encouraged an approach of cross-curricular to learning that encompassed all learning areas and facilitated connections making between areas.

Individual expression and creativity encouraged by them in many ways and are especially good at building self-esteem and self-confidence for a child.

The Froebel's woodwork influence spread internationally through the educational sloyd movement, initially in Scandinavia. Uno Cygnaeus (1810 to 1888) in Finland, was greatly inspired by Froebel's ideas, and in 1866 it became compulsory in folk schools to introduce craftwork through his work. Cygnaeus's intended to develop the hands of the children on aesthetic sense, practical skills and knowledge, and through the craft the process develops the thinking of children. He saw the work of his in Froebel's kindergarten as natural growth. Sloyd aimed in developing practical knowledge, through knowledge problem-solving ability of different processes of working and in learning through experimentation on how the work is evaluated and refined. At the forefront, was the woodwork but included other crafts like folding paper and working with fabrics. Hands working was thought in enhancing cognitive development and make learning more relevant, building confidence, and instilling respect for labor dignity. Both the ideas of Froebel and Sloyd movement influenced the introduction of woodworking in the United Kingdom as well as in many countries. Implementation was tailored in reaction to the current tool types and established techniques. This culminated in somewhat country to different country approaches to woodwork though maintaining a clear traditional core.

With the development of the global economy, woodwork lost popularity in the 50s and 60s, made it seen as 'old fashioned' and was found more appropriate for low academic children. Today we are starting to see a shifting trend of nursery environments and reception classrooms – originating with the early sector childhood. There's a revolution with noise! It's great to see that renewed interest and the growing one. The current prevailing thought is that opportunities needed by children for experiencing risk, to learn to assess self-risk rather than being over-protected. Children must learn decision making and judgments so they can protect themselves better in new circumstances. Now, Froebel's ideas are once again being adopted and there is currently an interest surge in woodworking and the establishment in the early childhood settings of areas of the workshop.

Chapter 1:

Importance of Woodworking for Kids

Woodwork celebrates the comprehensive essence of children's growth and childhood dignity. Woodwork encompasses play and innovation as the central elements of learning integration and development. Woodwork involves developing the 'whole' child core arrangements and, in particular, wellbeing and trust.

It gives children a sense of agency as they work with the heart, hands, and minds, a 'can-do' spirit that develops as their ideas to action are put by them.

Play

Playing and experiencing natural resources (open-ended) is essential to healthy development. Woodwork provides material for children to play, express, and explore their imagination in a convincing style. Children will essentially be 'tinkering' – involving both playing and experiencing first-hand and as a playful exploration tool it is defined. This unpressed materials exploration leads to deep learning kinds accomplished through play.

1.1 Connecting with the Natural World

Interaction with wood's natural material is provided by the woodwork, connecting the natural world to us and building material sensitivity. Meaningful is learning with woodwork and relates to the experiences and interests of the children:

Wood's smell and feeling, real tools using, natural material working, sawing and hammering sounds, working together of minds and hand for expressing their thinking to solving problems, using coordination, and strength: all together for captivating the interest of young children.

Woodwork assists in the development of:

- Children to create the connection between awareness of life beauty and knowledge

- The appreciation of the naturally occurring world's beauty/ nature respect /tree knowledge/sustainability.

- Awareness that we should produce and restore – establish an organization – and the value of producing and repairing rather than using and disposing of money.

- Authentic first-hand experiences of the instruments/materials of the real-world.

- Experience the beauty, knowledge, and life forms.

1.2 Freedom

Open-ended should be the work to allow children to play a leading role in their learning. Children will make their own decisions and choices. They will constantly develop skills and previous woodwork and learning building offers plenty of opportunity for the rich progress, multi-layered. Self-activity and free choice with adult guidance is important Froebelian concepts.

- Woodwork draws curiosity – the inquiry spirit

- Gives the first-hand experience

- Builds upon inherent motivation

- Engagement sustained-no limits of time -flow

- Child selections initiated-and option becomes continuous provision part

- Risk-taking under managed conditions/self-treatment

- Feeling confident and respected / use of tools

- Challenge graduated – with tools/wood –skill and trust progression

- Opportunity to fix issues in their jobs, time and energy

1.3 Guidance

With woodwork, clearly, we must guide the kids on how the tools are used safely, but also sometimes for nurturing their creative skills and skills of critical thinking as they solve problems in order to solve their job.

- Respecting children seen as strong learners

- Introduction of the instruments and the techniques

- The materials and tools respect

- Safety, risks and hazards emphasizing and discussion

- Ensure safe use continued

- Being offered as an additional hand

- Mutual relationship -the teacher resonating

- Interacting when it's useful in extending the thinking of yours – questions like open-ended / remember previous questions

- Expertise

- To facilitate reflection and assessment, and to share with others

- Suggest other dynamics – for instance, paper for expressing initial thoughts

- Constant vision area-in the-line overview

- Structural freedom – balance to allow for rich explorations

- Emphasis on unfinished commodity processes

- Individual and community

- Ergonomic tools choice and softwoods for helping you learn independently

- Projects grouped for facilitating communication and collaboration

- Humility and respect

- Ideas and thoughts sharing with others

- Mutual work reflection

1.4 Observation

There are several instances of schematic duplication that arise frequently that allow children in repeating and gaining trust and security. Observation assists adults to see what kids are doing and act in light of observations like these. This may be to help what the child is performing or could enjoy the continuation of the learning. Woodwork bench life offers rich opportunities for practitioners for making observations like learning and development, especially as thinking skills are shaped by the children.

Inner/ Outer

Another material is provided by wood for expressing emotion and imagination in this way 'making' the inner outer. Tools and wood arouse children's curiosity and interest and stimulate them for expressing the inner thoughts. It's a special mode of speech – mixing architecture with materials and working in three dimensions. The outer making process stimulates children in developing new inner feelings, narratives and ideas creation, questions and the solutions, and foster satisfaction and happiness. The external forces and sensations are internal.

1.5 Environment & Movement

Woodwork giving children suitable materials and tools, optimal that are for their ongoing development level it is essential not to institute frustration but allow them in building competence and confidence. For young learners, the imperative is the movement, and so rich is woodwork in many aspects of physical development like fine skills, motor skills, self-care, and hand-eye coordination, etc.

1.6 Child Expression and Unity

The human soul is nourished by creativity-it boosts our souls and goes beyond the earthly world. Human beings are fundamentally successful and imaginative, and by cultivating these in accordance with the universe comes fulfillment. We need to motivate the educational environment creation that involves practical work, direct material utilization. Learning unfolds by interacting with the universe. Play is an imaginative practice, and with it, children are conscious of their role in the universe. By creativity development, the opportunity is given to children to play, imagination expression and to represent symbolically. They can connect, and explore thoughts, feelings, and ideas. Complex material is woodwork in working with it and it provides constant problems – it's extraordinary that how strong it is to develop the critical and creative thinking of children as they solve problems and express the imagination. They develop perseverance when they deal with resources, and when they strive to produce the performance they desire. Woodworking fosters freedom and as children are accustomed to addressing challenges that occur through their playing, they feel secure in their abilities to solve concerns when they emerge.

Only children can learn what they're prepared for. Children are differently developing and must be allowed for learning at the developmental pace of their own. By holding the woodwork available to them, the stage of development that is correct for them will naturally gravitate – be it unpressed experimentation, pursuing their fascinations, structural repetition, or creation in mind with some purpose (narrative/abstract, representational, etc.). Other advantages are:

• The Knowledge Forms

• Information sources are coordinated mutually and work alongside other types

• Wood Knowledge as properties, material, trees, wood use

• Expertise in techniques and tools

• Computer skills and abstract reasoning

• The understanding and knowledge of science

• An understanding of technology

• Designing thought processes

1.7 Occupations Gifts

There's an intrinsic progression from gifts towards occupations-from playing wooden blocks to building with wood them-playing with the possibilities. Kids have fun in doing things with caution, and they take great pride in their achievements through enhancing mastery, problem-solving, and accuracy. But always bear in mind woodwork isn't about what kids do – what is created in woodwork gives new mind pathways as kids develop self-esteem, confidence, creativity, and skills of critical thinking, solving skills of mathematical problems, etc. At the woodwork bench, you can actually see children growing taller!

1.8 Beginning of a Noisy Revolution

As kids make wood they learn skills that will empower them to shape their world. Today, most children in most of the world's developed countries won't have the real tools working experience in all of their education. Clearly, this is a disservice for children because many occupations involve the usage of equipment skillfully. It is rarely found in elementary schools and most schools avoid resistant materials working. The need for more pupils to go into the research, production, architecture, and creativity industries is emphasized by the government. This left many kids with no experience working with the tools at all in the entire education of them. Clearly, a disservice to the kids is this and many are deprived of opportunity like that unless they're fortunate enough for learning skills like these in their home environment. To work like scientists, electricians, plumbers, carpenters, technicians, builders, mechanics, and dentists, etc., many children will need practical skills.

There're jobs in a large number having the potential to be professional with equipment plays a significant role, from the development of electronics and technology projects to the usage of surgical instruments in dental or surgery practice. Many universities have recently published reports related to prospective students who lack the skills set of practices that provide a theoretical foundation, skills relevant particularly to subjects like engineering, science, and product design. Practical tooling abilities are also incredibly helpful to all of us in our everyday lives, whether it's performing DIY designs, indulging in a hobby, or repairs making.

A changing landscape of reception classes and nursery schools is beginning – originating with the early childhood market. There's a noisy uprising! It is heartening to see growing and renewed interest marvelously. The ideas like kid's real tools working surprises many. Woodwork, fortunately, has a strong history of early education childhood dating mid-1800, but in the 80's and 90's, the woodwork was almost entirely eradicated with the burdensome atmosphere of risk avoidance and overprotection worries exacerbated by the culture of litigation. The current prevailing thinking is to provide children with opportunities for experiencing risk, to learn to assess self-risk rather than being over-protected. It had vanished almost in recent decades but now it is making a return, with revived enthusiasm from several colleges. In early settings of childhood and the primary schools, there's a dire need to promote woodwork. Children should attain from the woodworking rich opportunities it offers. Working with wood can be very empowering for kids.

1.9 Why should Kids learn about Woodworking?

There is really something special about woodworking. It varies very much from other practices. Wood smell and feeling, real tools using, natural material working with, sawing and hammering sounds, hands and minds working together for expressing their thinking to solving problems, using coordination and strength: all go together to captivate the interest of young children. It makes for a unique experience truly.

What about safety! Woodwork is, in fact, an activity of low-risk until the following of certain primary safety measures and appropriate instruments are used. At the bench woodwork, the behavior of children is exemplary-they are busy and doing things they enjoy. It's, therefore, necessary for children to encounter danger and difficulty in a regulated setting so that they can learn in making their own choices and assessments and thereby be able to defend themselves in different situations. This is a significant part of the growth of children.

Today woodwork providing teachers observe exceptional engagement level on a regular basis, with deep concentration and focus accompanied by perseverance and persistence with difficult tasks –with difficult problem-solving especially. For creative design and expressive art, woodwork is a delightful medium, and also it has the advantage of covering several other developmental and learning areas that provide a genuine activity cross-curricular. Developing in Mathematical thinking, gaining scientific knowledge, and developing technological understanding by tools working as they build. Most importantly, children are like engineers. Exceptional is a Woodwork for developing the creative skills and critical thinking of children as children experiment and tinker with the tools and wood possibilities. Subsequently, they move forward in expressing their ideas and work accomplishing. Woodwork isn't about what kids do – it's about the happening changes inside the kid. Woodwork has an impact on the confidence self-esteem of children and developing an agency sense – that mindset of "can-do."

Woodwork for children is a way of expressing their imagination and creativity. It's important that projects are not set by which all kids create a similar object. The children really remaining busy in woodwork secret is they follow their interests for creating their work and solve their own problems. When it is started, the overall discovery is more important and is driven by the children. By creative skills and skills of critical thinking building, they will lay the foundations for becoming future creative innovators.

Initially, the work of them is completely experimental-tinkering often with the tools and materials possibilities. Then children move on to show their creativity in a number of imaginative forms, creating research that they find fascinating individually. To more composite constructions they gravitate, from literal to more abstract and representational work.

The woodworking process combines design skills and practical skills. Design involves task defining, drawing up an action plan, deciding to proceed how, and improving and responding appropriately as the evolving work. The realistic ability or craftsmanship turns the designs to objects. As often fluid the work is and evolving as kids adapt, refine it, and change as it advances, go back and forth. Furthermore, older children might choose to create original sketches to better express their thoughts.

Many nursery schools' progress in woodwork establishing is having the effect of knock-on with growing primary school numbers already expressing some interest in expanding their stock. The possibilities are infinite for woodwork as a platform for creative design and art, and it offers too many links with other fields of study. It takes considerable time in woodwork establishing, but when the excitement of the children is seen by you and an extraordinary degree of concentration and commitment and the happiness and satisfaction in the work of them, it makes entire expenditure seem quite worthwhile.

Wonderful it is to see in the early years the growing passion for woodworking across the UK. Real tools working offers new experiences for children and includes all development and learning areas. Woodwork lets kids become tomorrow's innovators, sculptors, makers, tinkerers, architects, and engineers. Woodworking experience leaves a strong impression. They become part of children's DNA until they have understood how to deal with devices.

Wonderful it would be if we could have those experiences for every child. Watching, while they are on a woodworking project, children so intensely concentrated on experience, seeing their increasing confidence, the patience of difficulty, and endurance in failures face is a pleasure. Watching their creativity, problem-solving observing, and their pride seeing in their accomplishments is a delight.

As kids make from wood, they learn skills that'll allow them in their world shaping. Let's provide that valuable opportunity for all children.

1.10 Irresistible Learning

Anyone who's seen little children tinkering about with tools in the woodworking area might know how exciting it can be. Children show exceptional degrees of focus and commitment when being immersed in the construction. The benefits of woodworking to the development of children are evident across all learning areas, embracing many aspects of the curriculum. And woodworking from early childhood is now making a comeback.

1.11 The Return of Woodwork

Having been nearly eradicated owing to concerns of lawsuits, woodwork is now making a revival in early infancy. This indicates a more balanced approach to risk and the growing view that health and safety measures are in place to help children do safe activities, not deny opportunities. It is important for young children to experience risk in a controlled environment, and to promote the development of self-management and decision-making skills.

The revived curiosity in woodworking is another answer to our rapidly digital culture. We see a new generation of children trying to "swipe," until they are able to walk. Kids are surrounded by modern developments but their realistic understanding of technology has been limited by this. Currently, many children would never get the chance to utilize basic methods in their whole life.

Woodwork can be considered a great alternative, involving children with genuine tools and materials. In contrast to our prevailing culture of consumption and disposal, woodwork also gives children an experience of making and repairing. Worldwide, there was an upsurge in "design," as evidenced by the emergence of the "creator" phenomenon. Maker spaces and tinkering studios emerge in communities across the globe, offering environments where children can be adventurous, imaginative, and develop their innovative and logical thinking skills. It is truly extraordinary to see how much a woodworking session involves learning.

1.12 Learning and Development

There is really something unique about woodworking. It varies very much from other practices. The scent and sensation of wood, the sounds of hammering and sawing, the application of power, and teamwork all go together to captivate the imagination of small children. Visiting instructors, watching the woodworking field, often note the intense focus and dedication levels of the children, and they are amazed to see the same children still working on their creations an hour or two later. We see kids working with their hands, making structures, and working on inventions, but in reality, the true change occurs within the child — personal learning is at the center of the woodwork.

Woodwork is a potent medium for self-esteem building. Children are motivated and respected by gaining faith that they can function using real tools. They demonstrate satisfaction in mastering new skills and take immense pride in their creations. That sense of empowerment and achievement gives their self-confidence a noticeable boost.

Kids develop at their own pace with woodworking and find their own challenges. They should be moving into open-ended exploration once they have mastered basic skills — tinkering, discovering possibilities, and then making unique creations. Because children follow their interests, making what they want to do, they have the intrinsic motivation to persevere in problem solving and learn from errors. Their imagination, creative thinking, and problem-solving skills really thrive as they meet new challenges and conquer them. It's really extraordinary to see how much learning a woodworking session involves. It encompasses all developmental areas, encouraging confident, creative children with a passion for lifelong learning. Woodworking includes mathematical thinking, scientific research, technology development, a deeper understanding of the world, as well as physical development and coordination, communication and language, and personal and social development.

Essentially, woodworking is a 'win-win' experience: kids enjoy it a lot and stay engaged for extended periods of time and it provides a wealth of learning and development. The woodworking experience — involving hands-on, tridimensional activity — can be the key to unlocking learning for some children.

1.13 Ensuring Safety

Some teachers and parents are confused when children as young as three are exposed to woodworking, however, it must be stressed that when initiated and carefully supervised it is a low-risk practice. If you believe that young children are old enough to do woodwork, they are also old enough to learn how to look after their bodies and take responsibility with adequate safety protection. Some of the most important health and safety guidelines are as under:

- Wear safety glasses at all times. There's a very small risk with hammering that a nail might rebound toward the eye, or that an item being hammered might shatter. That risk is eliminated by wearing safety glasses. Small-sized junior safety glasses that fit comfortably on even the smallest of

- heads are now readily available

- Ensure proper instruction is given to all children regarding the correct use of all tools. Focus eyes on rough edges and machine lines. Keep a checklist of who learned to use which tool to ensure that all kids get proper instruction. Remind kids to keep woodwork equipment in the woodwork area.

- For sawing and drilling, a good, sturdy workbench with a vise is essential to securely hold wood.

- Sawing should be monitored on a ratio of 1:1 (adult to child). Wood must always be tightly clamped in a vice when it is being sawn. Be sure that no kids step in front of the sawing area while another kid is sewing. Immediately after use, the saw is placed out of reach (but visible to kids).

- Check splitting wood. Avoid wood which is very rough, splintery. Monitor edges of sand, if hard, after sawing. Warning: Splinters can be a source of blood toxicity. Guidance on first aid varies so check your local guidelines – common sense would suggest if the splinter protrudes then remove it. Either way, parents should be informed about splinters so they can monitor the splinter site for

- Possible infection.

- Ensure that all the nails and screws are then removed from the floor. A large magnet can work for this and volunteers will do the job willingly!

It is crucial that we hold our criteria of good practice strong so that we can hold the woodwork clean and provide all our children with these rich learning opportunities. It takes considerable time to set up woodwork, acquire materials and equipment, but when you see the excitement of the students, extraordinary levels of concentration and commitment, and the satisfaction and pride in their work, it makes all the expenditure seem worthwhile.

1.14 Recommended tools

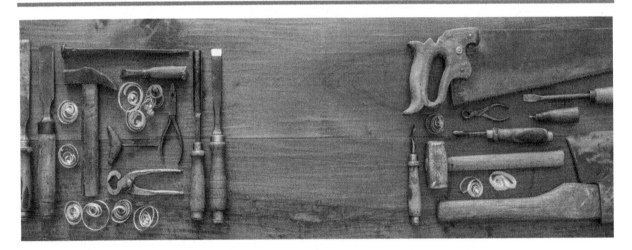

Having the most appropriate tools makes a huge difference and can reduce risk. The four primary tools used for woodworking are:

Hammer

The best hammer is a ball-peen hammer which is "stubby." These are all easily accessible now. They are designed to hammer out in awkward places for adults but they are a perfect weight for young children. They have small handles, so they are more controllable and have a wide hitting surface which makes hammering the nail easier.

Saw

For small children, saws that cut on the pull stroke are much simpler to use, are more controllable, and need less energy. These days there are a number of pull-saws available in the market. Advice is to go for Japanese pull saws-they are small, they have thin edges, and everyone who uses them is taken aback by how simple it is to use them. These are used to hold the handle with both hands.

Hand-drill

The safest hand drills are those with enclosed mechanisms, as there is very little risk of fingers getting trapped in the uncovered cogs. Ensure the work is clamped while drilling. Small drill-bits will not snap frequently.

Screwdriver

Use a screwdriver which is stubby. This is easy to operate short-handled screwdriver and the "cross" design ensures that the screwdriver is less likely to slip out of the screw.

Chapter 2:

A Guide to Woodworking with Young Children

Do you have some preschoolers? If the response is yes, then ensure that woodworking is implemented and that correct materials and equipment are made accessible for usage.

Woodwork is a perfect way to help kids work in their 'proximal growth environment.' How kids can do and learn is often expanded by the open-nature woodworking which needs children to be problem solvers. Kids also imitate what they see people doing, and through instruction, kids get great joy in being able to learn different things and do something they previously did not do.

Woodworking presents children with an outstanding play scenario to participate in problem-solving-a vital experience for children to build towards their future at an early age. Children must also improve eye-hand coordination, spatial perception, sense of direction, and learn how to properly use potentially harmful tools.

2.1 What if you do not know much about woodworking?

If you have little experience using carpentry tools why not take up the learning challenge alongside the kids. The most important thing when you just start is to take your time. Start with what you're happy with, and go there. Children can communicate more easily with you while you take your time, and that will boost their trust and you will soon be shocked by what they (and you!) can achieve.

It is not anticipated that any person should feel comfortable in this field of children's play, and should be able to hold a hammer, saw wood, etc. So it is vital to have at least one individual in the school environment that does, and who is willing to help guide, and encourage children.

2.2 Woodworking is not gender-specific

Indeed, gender is meaningless. It can surely be achieved by women/girls too! If they are enabled and encouraged, they can be as professional and as involved. In this area, both boys and girls will learn skills, competence, and trust.

It may be claimed that providing a well-stocked woodworking station/area renders the teaching atmosphere more boy-friendly, but the potential for both girls and boys should be made open and encouraging.

From an egalitarian standpoint, it's crucial not to deter girls from learning to bang in a nail, carve an item from a piece of wood, etc.

An excellent opportunity for children to learn from more skilled children

Older kids and kids more experienced in woodworking will be watched and copied by those less familiar and unsure about what to do and how to do it. It's not unusual for kids to encourage one another or spot on a woodwork bench while someone is having trouble with what they want to do and subsequently standing up to provide support.

2.3 Setting up

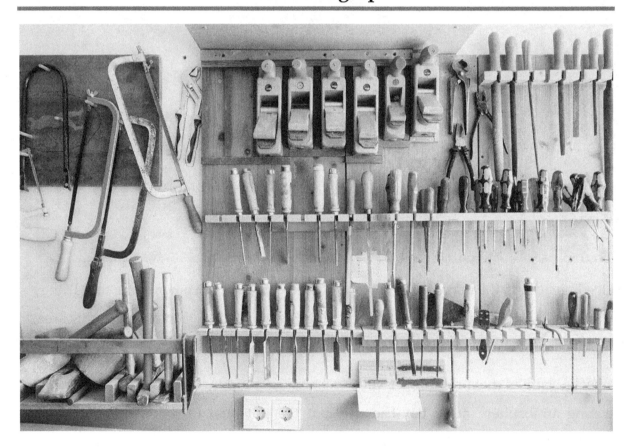

Parents do not need to worry much when it comes to helping their kids with woodworking. They can start off really simple.

WORK BENCH

It is not necessary to provide at-home for carpentry, a committed work bench but some kind of table surface is needed by the child. This is because kids are unable to saw, and a few of the things they want to do cannot be done on the ground.

A workbench is needed in early childhood centers to ensure that all tools and wood are kept together and made accessible. Based on the task children are performing, a 1200 mm x 600 mm workbench may be used comfortably for up to four children whether they are gluing and not sawing, for example, two children will be required to stand at the bench. For the children using it, the bench should be around the waist height. The bench should be around waist height for the children using it.

WOOD

It is necessary for the children to select and envision getting a number of different pieces of wood and strong supply. Workshops, some hardware stores, construction businesses, tree-cutters, and sawmills may be able to help and provide free off-cuts.

Do not use treated wood H4 or H5 as it contains arsenic salts that are toxic when converted into sawdust.

When everything else fails, what you will consider are branches that are 4 cm to 10 cm high. Branches that are 4 cm to 10 cm thick can be perfect for sawing and easy to handle in contrast with pinewood quality furniture. House clearance companies have frequently destroyed tables that they are happy to throw away because they have little interest. Pallets are often secure and can be easily removed with a pry bar and a hammer.

Large logs about 40 cm wide and between 25 cm -30 cm high create excellent single workbenches for children. When they work, they will put nails up in the top.

Drift wood while somewhat smoother than usual wood is perfect for learning how to saw.

VISES AND CLAMPS

Children don't have the power to grip a piece of wood and break it like an adult with one hand, so the first move is to show them how to use a muzzle or G-clamp to keep the wood still.

Some kids might need some help to get the necessary clamping force to stop the movement of the wood. Have them tighten the vice as much as they can, and then give them the final turn. Move on to the next stage, once the wood is securely in place.

Vises should be bought from hardware shops and can be locked to the bench to keep them from shifting. The vises of the engineer are preferable as they are much easier to attach to the workbench and prevent children from sawing into the top of the bench. Or if there's ample overhang on the bench top, a decent alternative is a pair of G-clamp vises. They are inexpensive and can be moved easily-two can be placed into line for large pieces of wood.

SAWS

It's quite a difficult task to use a saw when all you know is that you need to push it back and forth as fast and as hard as possible. That is a dangerous approach. When kids manage to actually start the cut off and get through the wood, they will saw the final cut through the wood, eliminating any resistance and the saw will start moving across the table driven by the weight of the boy. A backstop in the form of a plywood sheet behind the saw is perfect, as it can harmlessly stop the saw when a child slips.

Having the child draw a pencil line or mark on top of the wood is the best method to get the cut started. Place the saw at the mark, close to the handle, then draw the saw backward with a little force. Then, again put the saw on and draw it

back. Having created a groove of about 5 mm, get the child to push the saw slightly forward and backward until the groove is about 2 cm deep. And that's the aspect of lightness and delicacy.

They can apply themselves truly now. Remember that a three or four-year-old will require all their strength and body weight to get the saw to work, and will have no strength left to correct when they finally cut through. You can be prepared if you know what will happen next.

When the saws lose teeth, buy cheap saws, and replace them – which they will do over time.

PLIERS

Pliers are typically used to pick stuff up and to take items out. Pliers look very similar to scissors once the child gets accustomed to picking items up, using them like tongs.

Avoid using pliers with cutters, because if a finger is stuck this may be harmful. Small electronic pliers are the right size for kids and are accessible readily. Generally, they are about half the height of the engineering pliers.

HAMMERS AND NAILS

Adults may fear that kids can hit each other if they let kids

have hammers. But there's always a chance that kids could strike each other with certain items like blocks from the block corner or sandpit spades. It is a case of supervision, observing children and making sure hammers (and other tools) are used for the intended purposes.

Talk to kids about lifting the hammer no higher than their head height for safety reasons-this prevents them from accidentally hitting themselves or another child behind them.

Kid-size hammers or small hammers can be bought from hardware stores. Shortening a regular wooden-handled hammer length is an inexpensive and simple exercise, requiring a regular saw only.

Display and demonstrate the usage of the wrist to youngsters, then swing the hammer to strike the nail. When the child has developed trust in using the shorter hammer, they will continue gripping the nail and get going themselves.

When kids master starting a nail off inside a piece of wood, they can get a full-size hammer and achieve better results with a little more instruction. If necessary, a cloth peg about the nail bottom can be helpful in saving tiny fingers from the unnecessary harm.

The wish of choosing cheap panel pins must be resisted while selecting nails as these easily bend over. Long nails move into the wood, inflict harm to the floor underneath or the bench. Plaster clouts are inexpensive, and length is just fine. Seek other sizes too, when the kids become confident with clouts. You must avoid the use of large nails asthey are designed to be put in with a heavier hammer that a child cannot handle.

SCREWDRIVERS AND SCREWS

For little hands, a little fat crosshead screwdriver and screws fit great. An electronic screwdriver may be a nice tool, but they typically require a lot of time to charge like electronic drills.

DRILLS

Usually, cordless drills are used to drill holes and push screws in. Some of the cheaper 12-volt ones don't have much capacity. Many preschoolers may use a fair 12volt cordless drill competently but it's necessary to supervise again. The parent will remain within the child's range to ensure the welfare of the kid if required. At the bottom of the handle, cordless drills have a ton of weight which counteracts the torque, and typically has a clutch mechanism that gives some power over the force used. They do have keyless chucks with fewer places for tangling stuff like hair in – but long hair (on boys and girls, and adults) should still be pulled back into a ponytail while using some equipment, especially drills.

Another type of drill is a hand drill. There are two commonly available varieties-a plastic one with a winding handle that looks like a normal electric drill, and a geared one made of metal. Of the two, the metal is a sturdier model, but it's quite big, so it can be hard for smaller kids (although most 4 to 5-year-olds won't have a problem). The one made of plastic is perfect, although it will not last as long. The metal drill can accommodate bigger drill pieces.

A vice or clamp should hold the wood for protection while operating the hammer, as it requires two hands to work a hammer, whether mechanical or electronic. The maximum that most children can try to pierce a slice of 10 mm thick pine is about 10 mm. A 7 mm to 8 mm bit is usually fine. Educational suppliers normally market drill bits from 3.5 mm to 4 mm, but the larger drill bit has the benefit of avoiding the sideways pressure children exert on them. Often the wire nails are used as inexpensive drill bits, but they don't work very well.

Children may attempt to strike the nails with the drill, so parents should ensure to get the drill sharpened once in a month. When you make use of plastic drills, you need to check them regularly. Metal drills normally come with the promise of a lifetime. It is recommended to have a cheap cordless drill, but this is not essential.

Other accessories

In addition to the above mentioned tools, make sure that kids have the following:

Sandpaper

In order to ensure a suitable size for children, parents need to cut the sandpaper into half or quarters. Moreover, parents should supply smooth, rough, and coarse sandpaper to kids.

Ruler

All you require is a folding ruler or a rigid long ruler. This is useful to draw lines on flat wood for older children. This also helps to introduce older children to numbers that can be used to help them learn about measuring.

Carpenter's pencil

Children may draw a dot or a cross to mark where they'll hammer in a nail. Pencil markings may also be used to indicate when to begin sawing.

PVA glue

It is an important element since it helps kids learn how to join and fix things.

Paper

Paper is usually used for framed pictures, sails, and decorations.

Water-based paint and brushes

These will help instill creative skills in children.

Plastic milk bottle tops

These make lights and great wheels. In addition, a string for guitar strings, pull-strings to attach to the children's toys, etc., and anything else for decorations or other purposes such as foil, cloth scraps, fake fur, even leaves, could help children to improve and develop their natural abilities.

Socket set

Invest in a children's socket kit, and build items with nuts and bolts. Children will more conveniently use the socket set to secure the bolts than spanners.

2.4 Starting Off

One way to start is by using one type of tool for a few days or weeks at a time (depending on the frequency of use). This makes training the kids how to use each resource not only better but also simpler because you can also demonstrate many kids together. Wait before the kids become aware of the tools, and how to properly use the tools before adding more tools.

This is really helpful to think about what needs to be done ahead of time, especially if you decide to quit the woodworking area. The area is always in need of close oversight.

2.5 Communicate Safe behavior and rules to kids

Kids must be taught and ensured to comply with the following rules:

Tools should not be above the kids' height.

Kids should not run around carrying tools.

The tools must never be removed from the workbench area.

Kids must learn to use each tool perfectly. The children will need to be given a demonstration on proper use and handling of tools.

Children must use safety earmuffs to protect hearing.

Children should always be wearing shoes when working with tools.

Extending the learning and the fun

It's time to let the creativity run, and keep the fun going, especially once kids get involved and get accustomed to using tools. Below are only a handful of practical ideas:

Framed photos-Create photo frames for a drawing or a painting. Use cardboard for the back. Attach a string to the back for hanging the frame onto the wall.

Airplanes – You can start with 3 small lengths of wood. First, cut the wood to size for the main body of the plane, the back wing, and the front wing. Then you can add a propeller. This can be done by drilling a hold in the center for the nail. This will allow the propeller to turn easily.

Guitars – Use a flat piece of wood, and nail a long stick to it. Attach string lengths to the nails at each end. Then paint it with your favorite color.

Signs – You can maker street signs, garden signs, or name signs by first nailing a stick to a wooden board. Next, you can use a pencil to write on it the phrases like Stop, Go, Vine, Molly's House. Finally, you can give it your favorite color.

Push cart –The construction of a push kart is a perfect idea whether you or another person has any experience in carpentry or not. The 100 mm x 40 mm decking creates a perfect foundation. Wheels can be acquired from old bikes. Additionally, an old plastic patio chair can function as a seat. You need to help children create this fabulous push cart. To help the kids whenever they get stuck. Children will have a lot of fun. Plus they will learn some great skills creating this push cart.

2.6 Tips from the Parents of a five-year-old kid-How they helped their child to learn woodworking

My child always loved to help. He loves tools and he has a set of pretend play tools. However, at the same time, he's the perfect age to start some real woodworking of his own, so we got him woodworking set for his fifth birthday.

We looked at many collections of commercial tools for kids but none of them had all the stuff we needed, all of them had items we didn't want or need, and several of them were very costly, so we opted to put together our own kit of the woodwork.

Woodworking Set

We included the following tools in our woodworking set for Noah:

A kid-sized hammer – lightweight hammers are inexpensive and simple to locate in most hardware shops, make sure you have one with a claw so that you can use it to extract and hammer the nails!

Nails – they must be rather long and should have a large head for beginners

Drill bits along with a hand drill.

A clamp or vice – It helps to keep things intact while securing them. Moreover, it makes it simpler and better to firmly clamp stuff in place

A ruler and pencil for measuring and labeling – a tape measure are nice too, but more challenging for little hands to accurately measure.

Wood glue – It provides an easy way to fix small objects and decorations.

Sandpaper- We bought sandpaper of different weights.

We also purchased water-colored paints and/or markers for the project's decoration.

Various broken pieces that can be nailed, attached, or hammered-plastic bottle caps are simple to drill and then nail on, foam shapes glue quickly, beads stick and nail quickly.

Wood – you'll need to select softwood from a variety of woods. Many hardware stores can offer you free pine sticks, you may also inquire at construction sites (just make sure the pine isn't treated) or check for programs that include recycled art and craft supplies. You can also slice up small logs and sticks if you have firewood, and a large old lump of wood or a stump is a great and safe surface to hammer on or drill on.

We do have ambitions to introduce a handsaw but not until Noah becomes more familiar with the basics and is capable of handling such an advanced tool. We are also looking at a hack saw, especially the one which is small, easy to use, and capable of cutting a variety of stuff.

Woodworking with Kids

When they first began using the tools, they wanted a little amount of guidance and encouragement so it's crucial to teach the kids how to use the tools safely. This is an activity that, at first, required a lot of oversight, but as they became more confident and capable less oversight is needed – just a quick reminder about safety and being on hand to help out when it is direly required.

We gave Noah a large chunk of firewood. Then we taught (five) him hammering nails into that piece of wood. A broad solid surface indicated that he was just concerned about the nail and the handle, not about what he was hammering against.

To get the feel of hammering it took a couple of practice and a few bashed fingers, but eventually, Noah was pounding in the nails without too much difficulty. The parents should not hesitate to teach the children how to use the hammer's claw to pick nails too.

It requires a bit of power and skill but the digging of holes in objects is just something really rewarding! The children are always gathering various recyclables and saying 'may I poke a hole in that? 'For beginners, soft plastics such as lids and containers are perfect.

It is not often possible to bind pieces of wood together with screws, but it is simple to stick tiny parts and irregular shapes by applying some woodworking glue or a low temp hot glue gun.

Woodworking is ideal for the learning and development of kids. It provides numerous chances for problem solving,

situational perception, and the application of a range of abilities. Besides, woodworking is a fantastic creative medium for the kids.

Building something with just nails and wood can be a little difficult. Moreover, to make it the way you want is a bit more challenging. However, adding loose parts and markers or paints makes adding those little touches easy to really make your first project as you want it to.

All our kids loved hammering and grinding, and building using a platform they don't get to explore enough. It has been great fun to get into woodworking!

Chapter 3:

Kid Tools for Woodworking Kids

Early in their life, it's important to instill a work ethic in your youth, but it's equally necessary to show them how to love learning and learn different skills, and it all begins at home. Kids will still recall the first collection of devices that they put their hands on, the first thing that they learn. Yet where should you continue with all the instruments out there?

3.1 Ratchet and Wrench Set

Bicycles may just be the kid's link to the real world. Yet beyond that, they are a gateway to great exploration about how things function. The dismantling of perfectly good bikes gives a peek beneath the plastic veneer. The keys to disassembling and reassembling are ratchet and wrench. This ratchet and wrench package is perfect to disassemble items and bring them back together.

3.2 Bench Vise

If you choose to transform a wooden block into something more, you should be showing your child how to work on a desk. You will need a 4-inches jaw spread, the heavy-duty woodworking vise along with an anvil to help you whack everything into place. You can use this for anything from home welding and steel cutting to bar stock clamping. For optimum alignment, a swivel base is installed; the built-in pipe clamp is calibrated for working round stock.

3.3 Measuring Tape

Tape measures are sweet tools for kids. Tape measures are additionally important tools around the house. You can use it to teach your child numbers, and then fractions. The measuring tape above should be about right for children. The lock can be reached by small hands, and the blade extends a useful distance for small projects and play.

3.4 Block Plane

You will ease the square edges with a router for tasks touched by people hands — gates, tables, anything with a handle. But there's nothing like a low-angle block plane for children — and how to use it under adult supervision. Block planes, the irons of which split transparent wood curls at an angle of 21 degrees, explode with life lessons. Take off a little stock at a time; feel the tool through the work, and work best with sharp tools. Woodworkers often place planes on their side when they do not need them to shield the edge of the iron.

3.5 Work Clothes

There is nothing more beautiful and appealing than a kid ready to roll on a project in his or her cotton, in the context of home improvement and working with children. This one is made of 9-ounce, mid-weight, 100% cotton duck with double knees and elastic braces on the shoulder; the bibs come in as many sizes as there are kids.

3.6 Tool Pouch

Also in a tool pouch, there are life lessons: preparation, choosing the best equipment for the task, keeping track of your stuff — but the tool pocket for a kid is just plain fun too. This tool pack comes with hand equipment and protective glasses. Screwdrivers, paper scales, pliers, and a wrench allow it even simpler to walk into the shop and produce it. A kid who carries his own equipment, however, becomes a far more willing supporter.

3.7 Remodeling Hammer

The 12-ounce remodeler hammer, shown above, is perfect for the child's woodwork. Yet at 12 ounces, the item is just as small as it gets and as easy to handle. Kids enjoy banging on things, so why not set up a board with a couple of nails in it and let them have it? And when they're done, you'll take back the awesome hammer so that they might not be able to destroy or outgrow and use it for their own projects.

3.8 Hand Saw

A perfect way to teach children to make stuff is by sawing boards — securely. Perhaps it is not the best course to give them a worm drive of15-pound, but a small, nimble pull-saw Japanese-style is. You can find hand saws that have replaceable blades that are super primo and not-so-pricey. On the pulling stroke, they cut which is much simpler than on the pushing stroke cutting. And they are sharp, with no threat. Plus, you will be able to use them when your kid doesn't need them. They are perfect for projects of all sorts.

3.9 Kids Cordless Drill

They are, sometimes, alluded to as Gimlets. They lack a hand brace's strength and the egg beater hand drills' rpm, but they do seem to function well, especially in green wood.

Children have many toy drills. The thing is, they're just kids. When your daughter or son or has outgrown usage of pretend tools, it could be time for considering a practical device. A common choice is a drill but then you can select some impact driver for your child.

There are the following considerations why children should have some impact driver:

- Suitable for smaller hands

- Low Voltage

- No large chuck with large openings and a rugged textured ring – and safer

- No high strength required to tighten. They allow the use of a fast connector. Bits switch back and forth

- It's an instrument they will grow into, not some toy which will be discarded later on

Although it's tempting to buy the kid's favorite color matching one, you can get one matching the tools you may have on the battery site/service. When you don't have a preference for the brand, then go for their favorite hue.

Such devices also come without battery or are available with battery size choices. Continuing with smaller batteries such as 1.5 or 2 Ah is safer because they're both lightweight and lower in capacity. In fact, they are less costly too.

Buying a driver of real impact not only can develop up their abilities but also ensures that once they lose attractiveness, it can be relocated for use to the mom or dad's workshop.

3.10 Play Mat 4-in-1 Tool

4-in-1 tool available in the market is 4 electric tools for woodworking combination:

- Drill Press

- Disk Sander

- Lathe

- Jig Saw

Generally, it's quiet and convenient for a little machine. Your son will love shaping the segments of wood dowel on lathe along with the plywood thin sheets, provided in the package, being cut and sanded.

3.11 Kid Tool Belts

The workshop time part is related to learning of skills and the part is a little dress-up. Children tend to imitate adults. They enjoy doing what parents do and wearing what parents wear. Your tool belt, however partly mounted, would of course not suit the waist of your kid. It all comes off instantly. So much he/she needs to carry it that he/she ends up wearing it in both hands. A concern for safety it becomes after a few minutes because he/she is without free hands for protecting him/herself.

3.12 A bench hook for Kids

The objective of woodworking is to help young children in building things from the natural resource- wood. Thus a favorable bench hook can help achieve this objective and assist children to do 3 things.

- It can help kids saw more precisely. There is no doubt that accurate cuts give a better shape and look to finish projects. It goes without saying that success fosters confidence and pride.

- A bench hook for kids will assist them in sawing more

  effortlessly. This results in enjoyment building and thrill.

- It is a safe tool, and when used properly, it will not result in any sort of accident and keep the hands of kids safe.

3.13 Woodworking kits Toolbox

Often kids really don't initially have the tolerance to remain still when you're doing any of the pre-work to launch a little project. A few other days, you don't have the patience of prep-work doing for your young woodworker to build a tiny project. And that's where any of pre-manufactured kits could come useful.

While the prefab kit idea may often annoy the woodworker, it is often quite convenient to have quick access to take a tool off the shelf and work on it instantly with the child. You can get a toolbox that has a complete workbench and tools lines. They should be real but kid-sized.

3.14 Workbench for a child

The parents need to invest in a good workbench. This is because a fine workbench is extremely essential for a happy, safe, and secure experience with kids in the workshop, working. A good workbench should have the following attributes:

- Storage

- Dog holes

- Configurable rack

- Big work surface

You must have noticed that it lacks the presence of a vise. The aim should be to teach kids for securing properly their work as it helps in avoiding both frustration and accidents.

3.15 Workmate Kid Sized

To keep small hands off from the wood when they're sawing, drilling, screwing, nailing, and chiseling you must make sure to keep the work-piece clamped. Injuries happen when adults or children use a single hand in holding the work-piece.

If you're selecting your child's actual workmate to use, pick the one with the standing step. Not only it adds some height to your kids, but it adds to the bench the weight of them so it cannot slip. It has also a capacity of 450 lb., just in the case needed by you for your needs.

3.16 Saws for Kids

The protection will be the first condition before your child is able in handsaw using. The wood must be secure with helpful miter-box, clamps, or vises. Children will be instructed to place on the saw, both hands and one behind the back. This would remove nearly any possible accidents that could take place during the sawing process. With that, the next task is to select the saw that is just right for your kid. There are very few options, as with all woodworking tool selection decisions.

3.17 Hack Saws

Hack saws made for the metal cutting are indeed for children, the best starting wood saw. The teeth aren't too hostile and are thin. It makes launching quick, and going to and fro easy. The design of teeth is to hold up a decent abuse amount and yet offer a relatively good cut. The blade isn't quite large so it doesn't get as quickly lodged inside the wood as a traditional wood saw. Saw blade may be turned over as an extra incentive and it could be adjusted to either cut on the stroke of push, or the stroke of pull. Make sure to find one with tensions at both ends of the blade, not the ones flimsy where the blade end is not protected. Fairly plentiful and affordable are the replacement blades. When ready they are for real wood saw using, this one could serve its real cutting metal purpose and a tool it will be that throughout their lifetimes, could last.

3.18 Pull Saws

Pull-saws are present in a range of sizes and shapes, with teeth cutting on the pulling stroke. Typically teeth are sharper than conventional saws, so thinner is the blades, which means cutting is faster and easier with them. The carpenter type saws are recommended for use as they have one side of teeth. Double-sided saws are useful for the rip cutting with one of the side designed and the other side for crosscutting, but the existence of teeth on blade both sides poses a bit extra of health danger for youngsters. The one downside to the pull saws is if misused, sharp are the teeth and broke relatively quickly.

3.19 Toolbox Saws

Short are toolbox saws and have a stronger blade that renders them very robust in general. The handle of plastic lets it appear like a doll but it actually is not. Both the pushing and pulling movement cut the wood, so it cuts effectively and fast. The blade shield is safe and the teeth are covered entirely, and from children, it shields them who violently pick up their devices and put them away. It is a nice saw for children.

3.20 Coping Saws

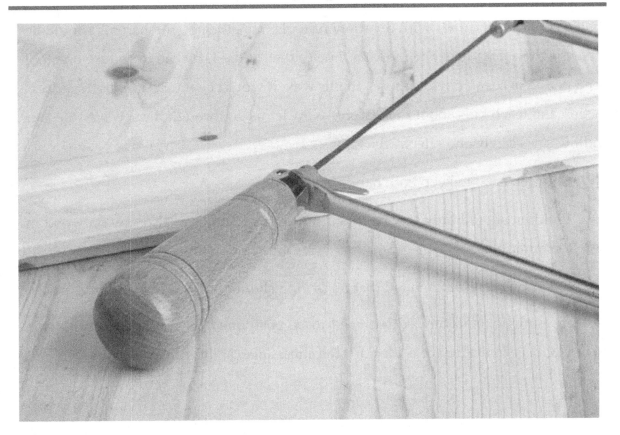

Kids can better avoid handling the jig saws or coping saws. When little kids used them the blades sometimes bind and crack. More time they take than the parents to know and learn how to handle these saws and a more careful hand in making them work. The mistakes are made by most parents of beginning their children with coping saw as they seem small and more convenient for the kids, but either of the saws shown above is a safer option.

3.21 Kid Tool Set Safety

While a set of tools comes with a variety of tools, nonetheless, the parents should be wise enough to introduce one tool at a time to their kids. They can introduce one tool after a period of seven days or more. In this way, it would be much simpler to address function and teach kids about **tool safety**. Now let us go through the specific rules for handling saws safely and effectively:

- Children need to keep both hands on the saw

- Children should only saw on wood in the vise. They can also saw on wood in the **miter box**

- It is strongly recommended that no sawing should be done on furniture

There are some tools in the set that need to be postponed for months or even years before you believe the device is ideal for the child's age, ability, and behavior.

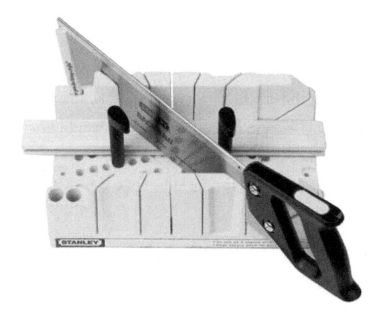

3.22 Tool Box step-stool

The Step N Stack-On toolbox will help your son balance on it when operating on the workbench of mine, and then put his equipment inside it when it's over.

These are larger than the most average size toolbox, and are built well to be safe for children or adults, especially when standing above them. It's estimated to carry as much as 325lbs. These stacks up just fine, you should buy them more. Additionally, its role as a toolbox and step stool, your son may even use it like a workbench and a bench.

3.23 Kids are young for some particular tools

A set of furniture-safe play tools is needed by you so kids with them can play in the places where the real tools wouldn't be suitable like inside the car, inside the living room, or at the grandma's home.

They require freedom to explore, while they aren't monitored and instructed; with a screwdriver, no hammering, no playing with a saw, no sticking the drill inside the mouth, etc.

There are tons of toolsets from which you can choose the best for your kid. Some of them are more realistic than others. Those looking more realistic also don't hold up and create some sort of confusion about what's real and what's the toy. They will play because it's a gift, if it's not a gift, they can't-or they shouldn't play.

There are a variety of children's toolsets. They both vary in the objects they've, and in the performance of the items. At one time, you can purchase a single tool which is an adult tool but accessible to children. More solidly they're made often a little, and for work, they're designed more than for some play, so they just work better when using.

Chapter 4:

Easy to Make Wood Crafts

Both your children and you will enjoy these easy making wood crafts; creating animals from wood clothespins and from Popsicle sticks the train tracks. Time to begin crafting!

4.1 Making of Train and Tracks

This track and train package will delight your child in playing conductor.

Provide your child 3 blocks of wood, a spool of wood, and wagon-wheel pasta six pieces to color. Cut rectangle chipboard for train tops and two train-window squares; let the child in pieces paint. Glue together the pieces as displayed, and wait until the chipboard is dry. For smoke, glue a cotton tuft onto the spool.

Cut a chipboard strip a little narrower than the tiny craft stick length to make the loops. Glue the mini craft sticks with standard project sticks at low intervals around strip and edges. Create a few tracks sets for the child to put together for extra fun.

4.2 Making of Tablecloth Clips Having the Ant Shape

Solve a popular picnic problem with fanciful ant friends and a flying tablecloth. These smart tablecloth clips become your latest favorites for picnics.

Start with painting black 4 clothespins. Thread a chenille stems, four-inches-long black through the 2 openings of a big button in black. Twist the ends and curl them where the chenille stems touch to form antennas. Glue the googly eyes under the antennae. Then cut black stems pieces in three inches for each of the ants. Help your kid thread all 3 in each clothespin through spring hole and adjust it in legs forming. The face is glued to each clothespin top along with two more black buttons. Then for securing tablecloth the clips are used and enjoy in the sun a carefree meal.

4.3 Making of Clothespin Giraffe

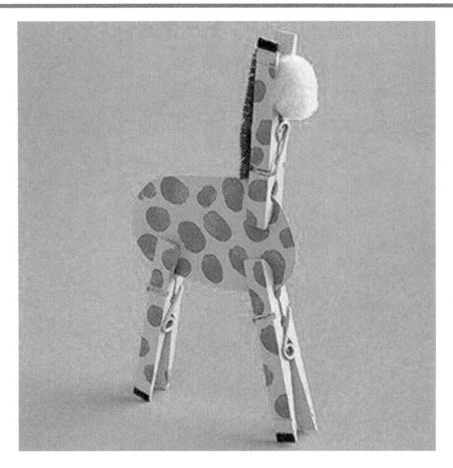

Thanks to the sturdy clothespin legs, this lovely giraffe all by itself can stand.

An oval is cut from the chipboard and paint it yellow. Also, paint the yellow three clothespins. Add the black paint, as can be seen, to each clothespin top. When dried the paint, let the child in using his fingers to make brown streaks on the oval body all over and the neck and leg of the clothespin. Attach on the body the neck and legs and stick it. The yellow pom-pon face is glued to the neck then attach a chenille stem folded along the neck back. This completes the giraffe.

4.4 Making of Airplane Clip (Magnetic)

You can enhance the increasing range of home-made art by constructing the airplane clip to your fridge's existing collection. Use this to show the new creative developments of your kids.

Paint one clothespin in spring theme, 2 craft sticks, and 1 tiny art stick in favorite colors of your kids. Once dry, craft stick is glued as wings on the clothespin top and the bottom, and the tiny craft sticks as the tail. A triangle shape is cut from craft foam and then glue upright it on top of the tiny craft stick. It's dried once, glue powerful magnets at the clothespin's bottom.

4.5 Making Barn of Craft Stick

Your child will find it easy to make an iconic barn (Midwestern) from craft sticks, painted one. Moreover, wonderful it'll look when hanged on the fridge in the kitchen.

Paint nine red sticks for craft, six white sticks for craft, and four white sticks for the mini craft. Leave them to dry. Let your kid make green grass and a blue color sky with markers or colored paper on a rectangular piece of cardstock. Support her then build the barn bottom by gluing vertically in the following design on 11 art sticks row: 2 red, 1 white, 5 red, 1 white, 2 red. Horizontally glue the white sticks over the top and the bottom and, as seen, connect 2 in the middle. Mini craft is glued in barn roof forming, sticking to the red cardstock. Fix the roof of the barn above barn to the background. A black paper rectangle is cut out and fasten this to the barn. For the look of hay, from a bag of paper take strips and crumple; stick to a black rectangle.

4.6 Making of Star Wand

Help your child create the craft table by using this star wand.

Let your kid paint with a silicone brush his/her favorite color on a wooden dowel. Allow to dry out completely. In glue draw lines from each point center, on a wooden craft star. Line in glue, sparkling beads, or sprinkle with glitter on the star. Wand assembling by gluing the bright ribbons and the dowel to the star's back.

4.7 Making Wind Chimes of Craft Stick

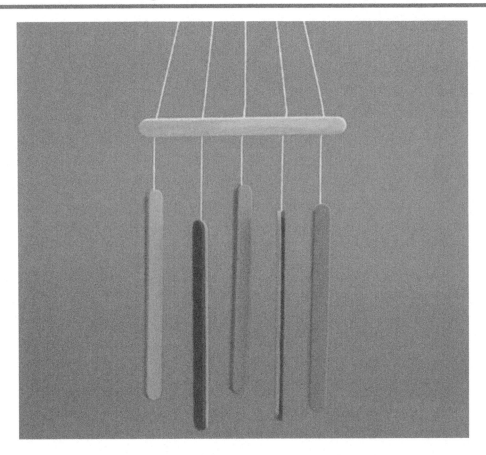

Hanging art sticks, when the breezes hit, create a gentle, beautiful tone — and they seem fantastic in wind.

Let the child paint ten art sticks and let them dry out. Place a glue line on 5 sticks backside. Sandwich a string piece between an unglued and glued stick; tie it with the clothespins to firmly retain the adhesive. Let dry. Drag glue over an unpainted art stick, horizontally lay it and hold, as can be seen, on the 5 strings (do not allow the sticks drop too far as they will tangle during wind). Use some other unpainted stick for topping and add the clothespins for securely holding the glue. When dried, put up the cords, then cut the surplus. Hang outside, and the wind would do its job.

4.8 Making of Large Wooden Dice

Challenge your kids to turn to original games like playing with large, multicolored dice — or just watch them having a ball in their preferred board games using the dice.

Let the kids paint on every side of 2 wooden blocks. Choose a number of shades of paper and punch the circles out as dice marks. Let the children count two dots sets on each block to glue in.

4.9 Making of Dragonfly Clip (Magnetic)

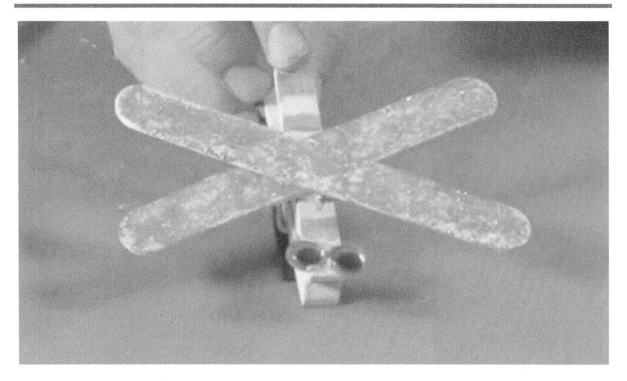

Display the artwork of your child by making this adorable dragonfly clip (magnetic) to stick onto your fridge.

Have your child paint his dragonfly with a few vivid colors. For the body, paint one wood clothespin and paint 2 mini craft sticks for the wings. When dry, put the project sticks in place on the clothespin top and glue. Attach to front of the clip, googly eyes, and add a large magnet at the bottom. On the fridge display it, and be very proud of your little one.

4.10 Making of Crab Hat

Feeling crabby? Cheer up with this crab hat that can be made by clothespin claws and paper bowl.

Paint one paper bowl and 4 clothespins red paper; paint white with 2 big wooden beads. Glue 8 thin 4-inch red cardstock strips to create legs across the bowl edge; when dry now fold them to the center for dimension. Together the clothespins are glued as seen and stick to the crab's front. Glue to the eyes, draw a black cardstock's mouth, and attach. The crab is completed by poking a hole at either side; elastic cords are attached to fit the head of your boy.

4.11 Making of Fishing Magnetic Game

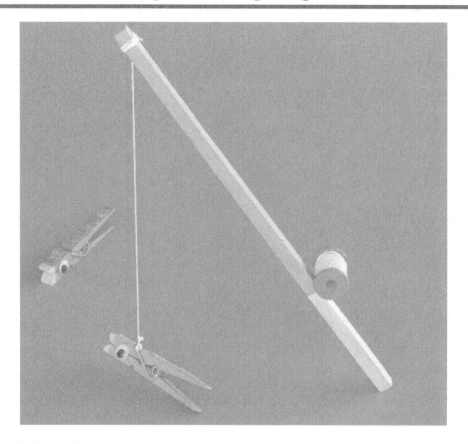

Provide the kids with immersive entertainment by using a few basic materials to create this fishing magnetic game.

Help the child paint his favorite colors on a wooden dowel in the square and the wooden spool, and allow them to dry. The white string is glued across the spool, then pin it tight to the dowel rim. A long string is attached to the distant dowel end and ties the opposite end, a magnet (from the hobby store's jewelry department magnetic barrel fit well). Render "cod" clothespin by painting with pinkish lips in bright colors. Let dry, the paint and aid your child to stick on the sequin scales and the googly eyes. Finally, he is going to be able to go hunting!

Chapter 5:

Popsicle Stick Crafts for Kids

Ice cream sticks or craft sticks are known also as Popsicles sticks, which are a common constituent in a household or any painting set that includes preschoolers and toddlers. There is no need to visit any special shop to buy these, because of having a vigorous nature. These rectangular wood pieces may deliver the bases for eclectic art projects and crafts and are easily available so that one can easily purchase these from the supermarkets, dollar stores, and even from office supply chains. These are available in the variety of shapes, large bags, either as simple wood or in color rainbows.

For snow days, rainy days, or when children need to do something, for this best thing are Popsicle sticks. Whether you need to craft the Christmas ornaments, structuring the buildings, drawing the rainbows, making the painting of your kid's favorite character. Children will use the Popsicle stick buying very quickly. There are many prettiest and simplest all ages kids Popsicle stick crafts that involve not more than paint, any glue gun, and imagination.

5.1 Easy Coasters

About coasters like these, the greatest thing is their usefulness indeed. Paint them you like or encourage your kids to paint these in their favorite colors. To practice the entire leftover crafting stick, pallet coasters are the best choice. Make patterns or make an entire set for every holiday. They propose whimsical party projects or fantabulous presents too.

5.2 Go Fish

This is a 2 in 1 deal project: once your kid and you end up the designing and their making, then you have a 'cards' deck to spend the afternoon games playing. How-to-create instruction holds some burner of wood, but if you do not have one, just fine will work a sharpie. Ask your younger child to make a design on the backside of 'playing cards' and you have to bring something new then, to fetch on airplane trips or along with long rides on the car.

5.3 Wacky Snakes

Once these full of color snakes are made by you, your children will enjoy the fun hours by putting apart them and joining together them again. They will be grateful to creators whenever they play. Your kid and you can style one long enough snake even to the length of the room of yours.

5.4 Crocodile

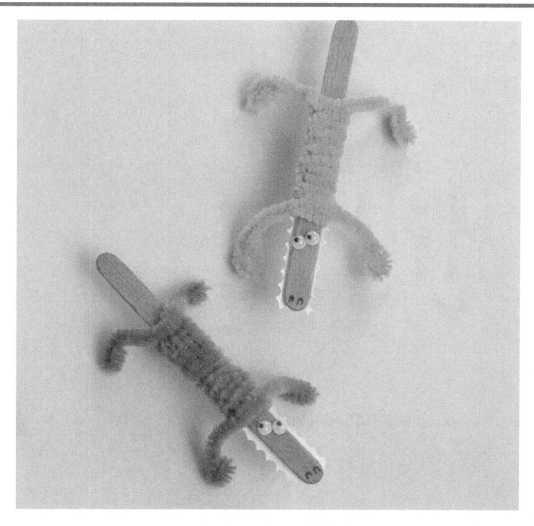

Time to smash the colored Popsicle sticks or green paint for such adorable and treacherous crocodiles. Fun, Simple, and easy has simple most instruction for these snappy reptiles that are certain to joy the preschoolers and toddlers. Desire to make it perceptual? Go online to educate your child regarding the difference between crocodiles and alligators. Or duo them with Popsicle sticks snake, or seek certain potted plants and start to play the Critters in wild.

5.5 Dreamy Creatures

Along with real-life critters, rivers, and swamps, these two myth creatures and legend offer excitement and fun to girls and boys in the making of this popsicle-stick unicorn. A bit yarn, a bit of glue, and some colored paper will assist your children in making magic crafts arise to existence. With these paper teeth and sleeping eyes, the monster does not have to be such scary! Make some wish, do not be frightened and enjoy with these really inspired unicorn crafts and monsters.

5.6 Picture Frame

Best Gifts for dads, moms, and grandparents are made of picture frames. With several items, you possibly have already at the home, your child and you may have fun together in making this such a distinct homemade frame. Several shortcuts have the easy directives and supplies list. Slack buttons make every frame an inimitable art piece. And by the use of a clip, it is too easy to alter the photo at your own wish.

5.7 It is a Wrap

Who knew that you can indeed bend the Popsicle sticks and shape it? Come to light it is very easy! Children of all age that love to follow with new trends, fashion and famous characters, that easy trick from 'Motivation Made Simple' will encourage them to design their peculiar jewelry. Preschoolers and toddlers can use paint for coloring or with markers, stickers, whereas grade-schooler can glue on the rhinestone in the entire sizes and shapes. For more sparkle, glitter is added or let your kid practice in making patterns. This is a lucrative activity for children.

5.8 Let's Fire!

You don't need the children to know that these crafts might be educational! Using straws of various lengths for launchers, kids can grasp the effort versus results though if they believe they are playing just with toys. And whereas the design might seem complicated in start, Steam Motorized Family follows simple directives that even less crafty parents can observe. Older kids by themselves might do this. Then organize the competitions to scrutinize the potent of launching cotton swab furthest.

5.9 Popsicle Nightlight

Creating the nightlight is not ever been easier. Pay thanks to the Artsy-Fartsy Mama that children can make their own wax paper, Popsicle sticks, some crayons, and some other things that can be a present nearby house with a handful of supplies. You may need to practice the iron in that craft for melting the crayons on some wax paper, so ensure the supervision of an adult and if needed take their help! Kids at bedtime will surely love this light new source.

5.10 Deceptively easy to make Flashlight of Popsicle Stick

Don't be scared by electronic involvement, instead, it is convenient indeed in that craft. Thanks to Entertainment Loving Families, that this is a prodigious STEM action for school kids or a recreational project to assist an individual to conquer the dark fear. The majority of already items are available at home that you need. If not possible coin cell batteries might be found pretty much at any medical store. For sleepover activities, utilize these for making shadow puppets.

5.11 The Puzzle

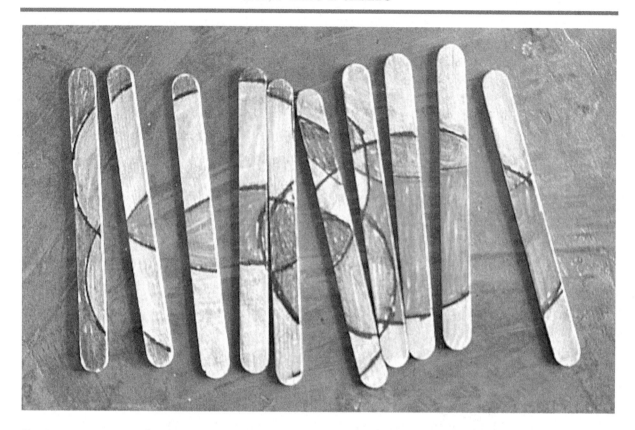

So many aspects there are to enjoy about this puzzle of Popsicle stick: it can be made simply and conveniently, the infinite designs to make, the way completed projects are swapped by the kids for challenging one another. The good qualities list is proceeding onward. For young siblings, older children can create puzzles.

5.12 Beautiful and Colored Baby Turtles

These younger children are too endearing for words. The way kids can swap their finished projects in order to challenge one another that softens the entire family's hearts. You will have a complete nest of prepared to hatch baby turtles by using three Popsicle sticks and some paint, yarn, and glue per craft. For every turtle, you can practice different color yarns or you can purchase 'self-striping' yarn. Even for preschoolers, to suspend off, pretty simple is this craft when they start.

5.13 Lightning McQueen

Disney and Popsicles sticks are picture-perfects. Popsicle sticks materials are easy to handle to craft and there are chances that the minimum one of the Disney character is known by your children. If this character is lightening McQueen, then you are very lucky with this naturally beach living craft. Use the craft sticks pre-colored or paint them. With some paper, glue, and scissors you are able to help the kid in racing at the track.

5.14 Monsters, Inc. Sully and Mike

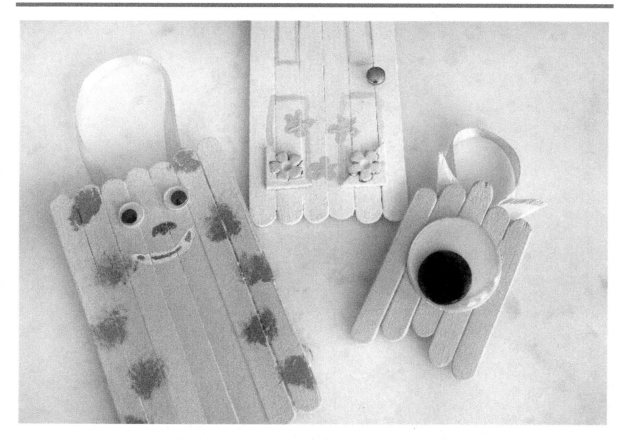

Monsters, Inc. if very famous in the house, check these Sully and Mike crafts out. This is exhibited like an ornament Christmas tree, they work like a door or wall hangings around the year. Don't forget: there are these guys for making laugh your child, not to cry.

5.15 Mini Mickey Mouse

This project is to fasten and save the tour with your family to Disneyland or Disney World. To use Popsicle sticks, paint, and glue, it is not necessary to be some professional artist in animation for making this lovely craft of Mickey Mouse. Reveal this for surprising your children to Disney Trip by using this or let them do it before you while they prepared themselves for a lifetime event.

5.16 Mickey Bookmarks

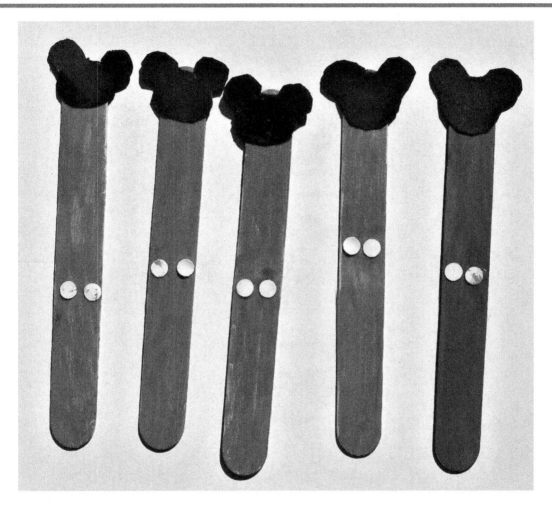

Here is the best idea for preparing this bookmark craft Mickey Mouse for little kids in advance. To turn them to Minnie Mouse, enhance the little pink bow. These very simple bookmarks produce the souvenir perfectly even if the family has not been to Disneyland yet. Bonus: bookmarks like these can be doubled for toddlers as stick puppets. And do not be astonished, if the older kids swipe some of them for marking their places in the middle-grade book's chapter.

5.17 A Snowman

Covering the Popsicle crafts Disney-related comes the favorite of everyone snowman! Bring to life the Olaf by this endearing task from Craftionary. Here, no imagination is required: entirely you only require making the Olaf for your child are basic supplies of crafting you can easily get from any kid's crafts and kit arts.

5.18 The Treasure

If your kid has an interest in collecting the things or what kind of child he is? Then you'll certainly want to see this Treasure box of Popsicle stick from geniuses at the Powerful Mothering. In the baking tray place the materials for minimizing the mix-up and now allow the collector of pint-sized to go to their treasure box for those all pieces and bits they collect.

5.19 Multipurpose craft

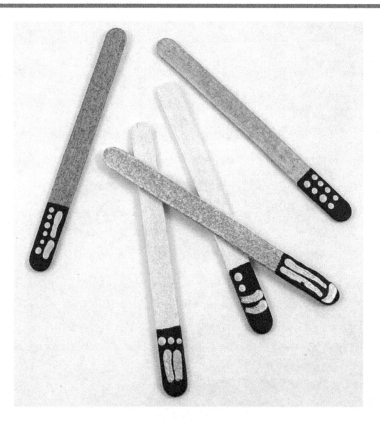

If you're exhausted from back home children's festivities with splendid bags containing the useless plastic toys vulnerable to break in mins. Then with these convenient Popsicle stick lightsaber becomes everyone's favorite class mom! After the young Jedis are finished with a lightsaber war, these sticks as bookmarks can be utilized (of course in their beloved Star Wars satire!). Lightsabers come with almost every rainbow hue and there are a variety of lights for going around.

5.20 A Simple Puppet

This is just the thing of Star Wars for parents that wanted to bring their children to the exciting saga as quickly as feasible. Just Popsicle sticks, black marker, and a paper plate, Yoda puppet couldn't be simpler-or- sweeter. You can build the beloved swamp dweller Dagoba in only a few mins! A few googly eyes can surprise even those sitting in elevated chairs.

5.21 The Rainbow

Rainbows are striking colorful and sweet they are prompt hit to almost every kid of all age. This beautiful rainbow-stirred Popsicle sticks designs are very basic and can be created by pre-colored art sticks or by plain ones, while your kid and you can paint it together to give it a wonderful appearance. Feeling spooky? For some ombre like effect, change the paint order to create a distorted rainbow, or choose various shades of similar color. These will definitely brighten the rainy afternoon with sparkles foam paper clouds!

5.22 Abstract Art

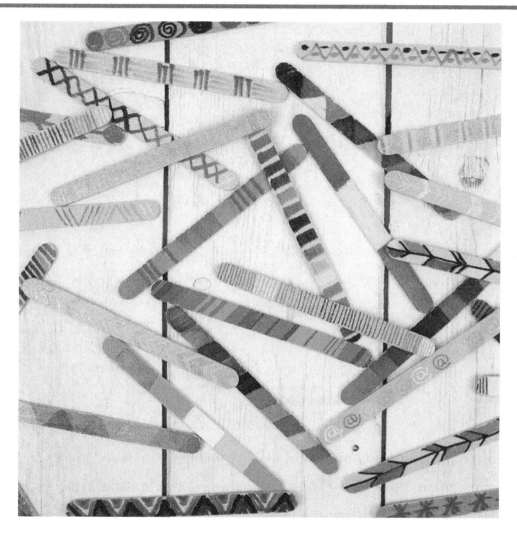

If it is time screen-free at your home and the older children can't bear even other board games, get the markers out, Popsicles sticks, and paint for this imaginative project. No child is big for this worthwhile project and it is easy to combine the customized sticks of everyone into one huge piece once they're finished. This is indeed a collaborative effort that brings the entire family members together for entertainment, recreation, and time for creativity!

5.23 Easy to Make Diary

If your kids have made already mound of the DIY stamps from wood pieces, button, or cork, then use them! You can easily assemble these Popsicle sticks in a book, then which can be ornamented with any stamp made by your child – or with entirely new designs that can inspire and motivate kids! They fit well for the teacher presents or can be used just to make your child stay in bed until they fall asleep. They can use it to scribble or color before going to sleep.

5.24 A Colorful Popsicle Art

Like the honied baby turtles simple is this craft and only limited by the imagination of your child. If your child has outgrown his baby animal age, give them some yarn and Popsicle sticks to make some crafts influenced by the summer camp. Although in the 1970s it was called a "God's eye art," still a pleasant and swift project are these. Self-striping and colorful yarn for these is substantial, or you might use stored away yarn scraps for the easy peasy project.

5.25 Daisies of the spring

Bring various color on days like snowy to your home, or rejoice spring with such colorful daisies. Spend a day making the whole garden, or some beautiful bouquet to offer as a present. Using mason jars at the fireplace mantle as vases or take them in use to brighten the room. For tiny fingers, these are simple enough and don't need lots of customary or distinct materials. Here are the perfect kind of crafts for your children to enjoy the spring season!

5.26 Easter Bunny

If there are Easter Bunny baskets every spring at your home, why not give him in exchange for something dainty? Just as children love setting up cookies and milk for Santa, try to make baskets of these Popsicle sticks. Or just do it for carrying Easter eggs throughout the building. These baskets can double for a prodigious non-Easter usage as party favors coin collectors, class projects, or holders.

5.27 Butterfly in Sky

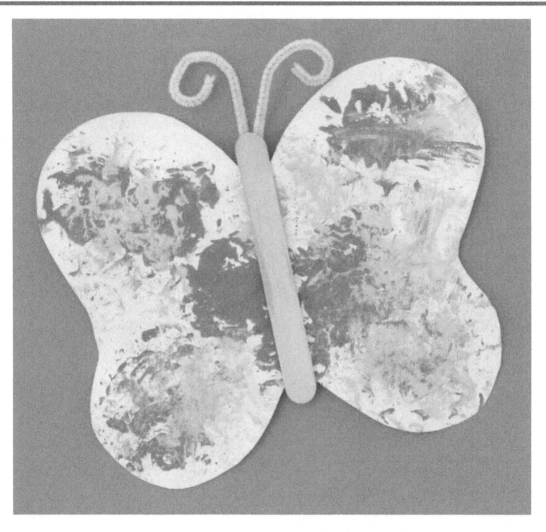

On the list, the foremost butterfly project is uncomplicated for early kids, but recreational for early grade schoolers and preschoolers too. It's encouraged to use those construction paper fragments left over when your kid is only using his favorite colors. Do tape a kaleidoscope for a springtime onto your active room walls or suspend these from the ceiling in the child's bedroom to encourage their thoughts to fly!

5.28 Fairy Butterfly

The next butterfly of the list generates a lovely butterfly right out of folk tales utilizing art feathers and googly eyes. Soft and nice, don't be shocked if they can finally keep your kid company in bedtime! They construct a perfect springtime experience for sleepovers, birthday celebrations, or for amusement every time of year! Hang up some of the above-listed butterflies from kid bedroom's ceiling of your for a stunning effect!

5.29 Bird House

From butterfly to the bird crafts, here's a simple house for birds that can make your child gratified of all the season. Just four items are required to make this lovely birdhouse. What happens on rainy days? Create some and reserve for them, when the sun again comes out. Your child would be so happy to see birds come in to eat from a nice wood craft created with his own small hands! Seek to create this to help kids hold a list that contains the record of every bird they see visiting their house of the bird.

5.30 Buzz, Buzz

We can make the continuing spring craft theme by using Popsicle sticks, but make sure to construct these pollinators of the backyard for spring Daisies. These small children are so endearing that you are not even going to care about getting upset. It is a simple project to create which children would love to do with the assistance of the parents. Who knows? You could end up in your active room with a whole hive, buzzing around and soften your heart!

5.31 Picked Only For You

Here's a fun addition on the custom of offering Mom coupons on Mother's Day: a Popsicle stick of flower coupons bouquet. Even you can keep these flowers year-round in the "vase!"

5.32 Stars and Stripes

For the Flag Day, July Fourth, or whenever your children feel the devotion to their country (the Olympics), stockpile on the white, blue, and red paint for American Popsicle stick craft. Also, add to top a ribbon for a Christmas tree entirely American on July 4th or as an ornamental door hanger!

5.33 Summer Lazy Days

Exclusive of the beach, what is summer? Allow this keepsake to hold memories alive during the year. Fill up a jar with sand halfway, ask your child to pick up some minor shells from the beach. And you've found a seaside memorial to warm you during those winter months of the cold! Wherever you place these at your home, your kid and you will still be reminded of sandcastles, sunlight, and swimming.

5.34 Pencil Holder

School time again has to come into a child's life. Help them move from summer entertainment to the books, and also assist them in gaining knowledge with these colored pencils. Through customizing the shades, stickers, and ribbons, your kid can hardly criticize (... well, maybe worry marginally less) about something so lovely where he could keep his pencils during homework time. If your children are very young that still have homework, use paintbrushes or these markers in your kid's art nook!

5.35 Let us do some magic

When the greeneries begin to grow and then temperature falls and stores store whole aisles filled with pint-sized candy bags – it's time for arts in Halloween and crafts. Commence with these fun little witches and let your children enjoy creating this not-so-scary Popsicle artwork out of cardstock or violet paper? Go for your witch with a typical, green face! Hang these in the windows to hail trick/treaters, also you can stick them to a wall for a Halloween party that's not scary!

5.36 Gingerbread House of Popsicle Stick

Interestingly, these gingerbread houses require no baking, which is certain to become the new desired tradition for your family. You can allow the imagination of your child's motivation to purchase any adornments that their hearts wish. Set it in the Christmas trees, on the wall tape them, or sum it to the Christmas town. Make sure they don't try eating them!

5.37 A Cocoa Cup

Let your kids warmed with those hot mugs chocolate after some long winter-influenced crafts day. No water timing cups in stirring milk pots on stove or microwave. And calorie-free 100% is this hot chocolate. Paint and ornament with any paint your children love and make certain to add abundant marshmallow cotton balls to the head.

5.38 Winter Wonderland

They are attractive and can be rendered as special as true ices. They're so much enjoyment that your children don't want to just make one and keeping busy them with hours of crafting.

The only obstacle that keeps the kids from making more would be running short of items of ringing bells, glossy pom-poms, glue-on beads, and lots of colors! This art truly is a guardian to cherish every winter.

5.39 Let us make doors from Popsicle sticks

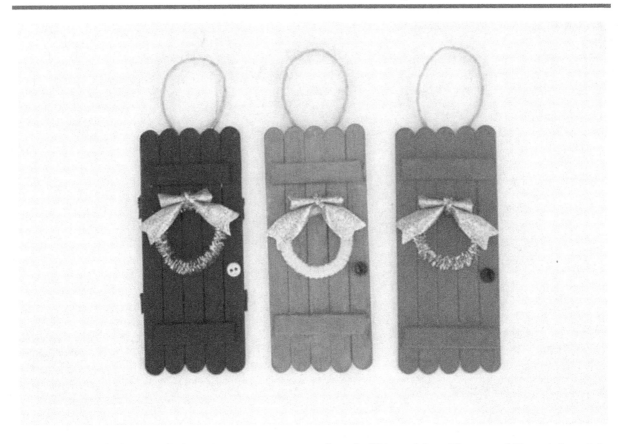

For some Holiday craft, here's an uncommon but brilliant idea: Doors of Popsicle stick.

Just try building these fun doors for your kids while the house is before now full of Christmas trees, reindeers, jingle bells, and snowmen. Pipe cleaner adds a nice touch to those little doors as wreaths that could be rendered to suit the real one in your home or make them available to your children to let them customize.

5.40 It's Downhill All

These Popsicle stick wooden sled ornaments are identical to but exactly not the above Popsicle stick doors. They're just right Christmas tree year for a family after a year, with that old-fashioned feel. Let all children make their particular, and give him Sharpies to let them mention the names on sleds. Once the season has ended, gently put these away so one can spend the rest of your life with these nice keepsakes!

5.41 The funny Elf

This is not merely to be seated on some shelf! We mean this little guy! Popsicle sticks elf's adorable face can move anyplace in the home needing some cheer for Christmas. On those winter-break days, your kid and you will enjoy a Christmas decoration together at home. This fella is made irresistible due to these great large googly eyes and the ruffle of pom-pom neck certainly makes him pop. Rather than using simple Popsicle sticks, encourage your kid to paint his elf in color wanted by them!

Chapter 6:

Wood Crafts That Can Be Made By Kids At Home

The most beautiful things that can be done with the little ones are probably wood crafts as they're such a great activity of teaching and allow children for exploring nature as well! Take the children out for some walk for finding wooden objects of various kinds such as branches, twigs, or leftover wooden scraps — and during the walk teach them what are the different wood uses, that is, making paper on which we draw and write, building structures and home in which we live, making equipment of sports such as bats for baseball and also furniture!

With those kids wood crafts, you can encourage your child. It will inspire your kid to go out and appreciate the natural environment. This list begins with the simplest projects requiring the few materials and some tools to none.

6.1 Twig ABC's

Literally speaking the simplest in the full list is this project. Preschool Toolkit is for preschoolers intentionally that are still in the alphabet learning phase and has a twigs list exactly your child and you need to make A to Z all letters. Turn a routine stroll in a learning opportunity in the park! You can cut or break the twigs easily to the length need by you if you have to. Does the child know the ABC's already? Start practicing with easy three-letter common words, and help your child reading and writing these letters!

6.2 Glowing Wind Mobiles

Here are another fun and the quick wood project can be enjoyed with any age child and with very little extra materials. Not only can this project build a lovely smartphone to hang outdoors, but it teaches children also fundamental technical principles such as compression and tension. A great way is this for using up yarn scraps that you might have around as a bonus. When the child of yours grows up and becomes a very-famous engineer with this easy craft, they'll thank you because you inspire them!

6.3 All Together Tie it

With this simple but fun project off art, that is perfect for ages of all, a day at the beach can last forever. No local beach? Go to your own backyard for a walk or for collecting different lengths of sticks. You're never going to have to get your child to leave that all driftwood and they're going to get a tangible reminder of an enjoyable beach day!

6.4 Use leftover pieces to make creative artworks

Do the remaining wood pieces from various art ventures overflow your house? Here's the great idea of using them all in an easy way! Your kid will have fun drawing and coloring it, and you'll love to see their imagination taking flight with the endless forms they will bring together with wood pieces.

6.5 Nature Royalty

What kind of child doesn't like wearing a crown? Julia Donaldson's book "Stick Guy", if loved by your family then your children have almost definitely collected sufficient twigs to create this simple and cute stick crown influenced by the leading character. Easy in helping kindergarteners and preschoolers, it's a way of fun for kids for making something that they can show off by wearing it

6.6 Easy Peasy Stick Man

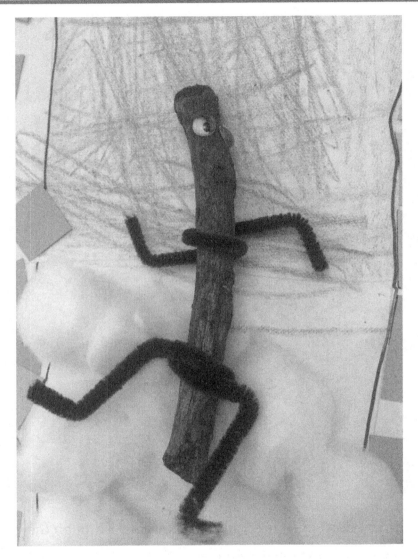

This project lets the child's imagination run wild with some pipe cleaners, few cotton balls, googly eyes, construction paper, and glue. On the wall, hang it up at the favorite reading corner when you're done, above the little one's bed so it can be seen easily by your kid while you're reading or next to a chair!

6.7 Nature Made

So easy is this craft you don't even need any tools or glue! Through this inspired craft turn the entire backyard of yours into paintbrushes. Small twigs are the brushes handles that are covered with something of nature that your child likes. All ages kids will love how much these can be made by them in one evening. And the great part is these can be used by them to paint art inspired by nature!

6.8 Reindeer Craft

No special equipment or tool required for this cute little Reindeer craft Red-Nosed, once again. In fact, besides some clay, in your own backyard, you'll find everything needed by you. This activity is perfect for little kids as the clay can be rolled by them in hands to create the body of Rudolph or for their antlers and legs, attach the twigs. If a red color seed isn't available for "nose", just paint it!

6.9 Simple Driftwood Kite

If your child has collected their favorite twigs after some long hike with the family – or after 10 mins in the backyard – then you should go for this kite craft. Wooden beads will be needed by you that your child and you can paint easily, but you'll do whatever beads laying around you. A perfect activity for preschoolers and toddlers is this to improve the motor skills of them, and to learn pattern formation for high schoolers!

6.10 Mermaid Friend of Mine

A quick visit to the local craft shop will help to collect everything need by you for helping the child build these wooden mermaids from spoons. Children can make a mermaid with different lengths and colors yarns which looks similar to them. Or, grab some crazy colors to create mermaids with green or blue hair!

6.11 Magic Unicorns

Always popular among the children are Unicorns, so they're nearly everywhere these days! Just as you thought there might not be a single unicorn in your child's life, this cute little unicorn project comes here. These fairy creatures, along with mermaids of a wooden spoon, as shown above, make fantastic group games, puppets, or even fun artworks to hold forever. Using the creativity of your kid, you can pick your selection of materials for creating a whole band of beloved creatures.

6.12 A Lovely Wooden Frame

Young kids like to make gifts for the people. For Valentine's Day, Mother's Day, or because, it's not easy to ignore this quick to build the frame. With some of the craft store's cheap, readymade wooden frames, plus few paints and a cookie-cutter of heart-shaped, your kids can have very much fun dipping their thumbs in the paint for making this craft! It's shockingly easy, totally worth, and kind of messy for an eternal reminder when thumbs of your kids were that small!

6.13 A lovely Photo Frame

Try out this stunning frame influenced by nature when dreaming about picture frames as presents, especially if you can't take another macaroni bracelet or a Play-Dough cup. You have everything you need to build this beautiful and sentimental picture frame with some inexpensive items from the nearest craft shop and a trip outside with the preschooler. Add a photo of your child to use it to frame some of the favorite art of theirs for the living area!

6.14 Abracadabra!

Here comes a beautiful and easy way to make magic wands for the budding wizards, magicians, fairies, spell-casters, and witches. Children will easily turn themselves into next Hermione or Harry Potter with nothing more than sticks and ribbons! The best aspect of this project is that every child can get their own completely personalized wand depending on which twig they want most and how it is decorated by them. Just don't let the younger siblings turned into toads!

6.15 Here comes the winter with Snow

These magnificent snowflakes are surely going to be famous during the long months of winter when it's too cold for staying very long outside. The twigs must be collected during the season of warmer, or pick up some when it's time for the children to sled. Recreating a wonderland winter in your home is fairly easy. Your child's space will become a palace full of ice like Elsa's with the addition of a little glitter.

6.16 A Colorful Mobile

When hanging the inspired designs of your child around the home, make sure to build one of those eye-catching mobile cameras. This project incorporates only some things that you can purchase at any of the craft shop, which works with children of virtually any age. If the kid only needs to paint some sticks, is enough old to connect them together, or to a hanging rod attach them all, they can certainly have fun choosing colors and creating shapes!

6.17 It is time to sail

When you've some yarn or string and a glue gun, it doesn't matter how much twigs are collected by your child, you can build an armada of sailboats! With some application of your creative abilities, your child and you can spend the time you wanted as playing shipbuilders. Place them on blue paper and take a sailing ride, or go for an expedition around the globe!

6.18 A Keepsake that can last forever

You might have a friend who likes cutting wood or you may yourself do it. Perhaps you only enjoy purchasing pre-made crafts materials. However, you get them, collect some slices of wood and paint them, then be ready for making some valuable keepsakes with the kids. This project best part is that you can finish it in any colors you want, and many handprints you can do as you like, or you can go for one just per slice!

6.19 Sliced Wood Ornaments for Christmas

While collecting wood slices, make sure in saving some to decorate the Christmas tree for some of these festive crafts. This is a cheap way for making fun ornaments for keeping or giving as gifts. You should allow the imagination to run wild and draw on as many imaginative ideas about how and when to create like images of Santa, snowmen, and monograms. As your kids grow up, you'll love to find them in your bin's holiday decorations. It will also remind you of the time when you created these with your kids when they're pretty young!

6.20 Build a Racetrack

Wooden plain blocks are the cornerstone for this amazing project which will keep children occupied for hours! Only sand and then paint, then let the kids build and restore their car toys and trucks toy with an unlimited amount of race tracks. The more tracks you create the more shapes children can create. These can be used indoors on some days like raining, or children can go outside on a sunny day to play!

6.21 Nails and Hammers

Try out this cute porcupine project if you believe your kid is ready for learning how into the wood, hammer the nails. Add a bit paint to the porcupine's nose, and a plain, triangular woodblock turns into a cute little thing, like a doorstop. You can give your kid a clothespin of wood for helping them holding in position, the nail, and this is a brilliant idea for helping them learn the proper use of a hammer. This is one that children would ask you to allow them to do again and again!

6.22 Create Heart Strings

You can trust this friendly preschooler project when you've got your hammer and nails out to support your child to make another beautiful art. Either you can let them in hammering the nails in a shape pre-drawn, or hammering them as you like, depending on your child's hand-eye coordination (and your nerves!) Then give the child a thread or string red color for hearts! You can then let them wrap again and again around until they've got a unique artwork!

6.23 Create an eye-catching Spider and the Web

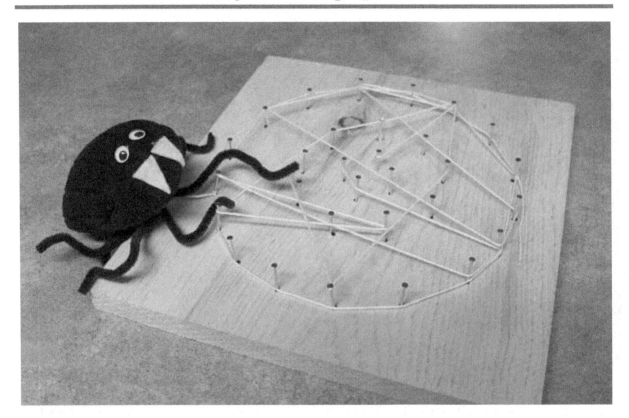

It is not finished yet! Here's another thing that can be done with a hammer, some screws, and some string or rubber strips. The pattern is drawn firstly on square wood slab and, if you're sure they're ready, let the kids follow the pattern of nails hammering. Kids then build a spider's web using string or rubber bands – and then cut it apart to construct fresh webs again and again.

6.24 An easy to Make Catapult

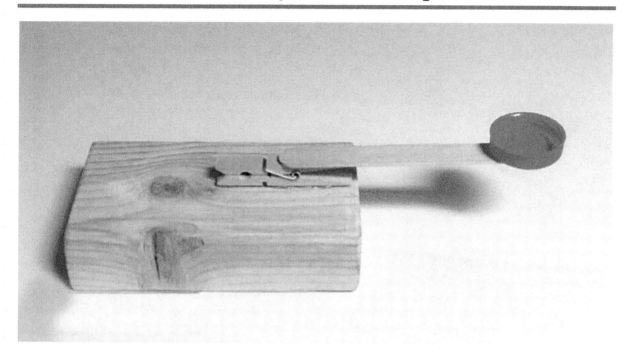

Half the materials required to build this catapult ideal for small children are a basic wooden block and a clothespin of wood. You should let your child use balls of cotton as projectiles and that is a perfect idea to save the furniture from the projectiles! Children will use paint or markers to design their catapults whereas you have to monitor and control yourself entire hot gluing. The only problem now is: How to clean all those balls of cotton?

6.25 Create a Big Catapult

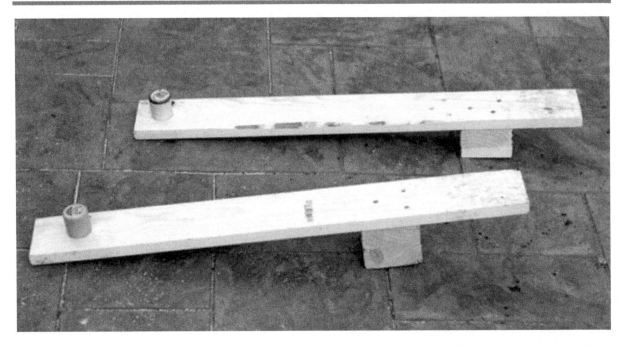

When your children have grown past arts clothespin and crafts clothespin, take them for some 2x4s to some hardware

store and saws. You can help them to build a larger catapult version. The older grade kids can measure, carve, hammer, and screw a pair of wood blocks and planks together under the supervision of parents. Choose small, items having lightweight to help them make this catapult. Once they're done, you have to make sure that they don't target the yard of the neighbors and friends. This is an artwork definitely meant for the outside!

6.26 Topsy Turvy

For these old-fashioned toys, adults certainly need some preparation to do, but kids can always have a lot of fun drawing and working! You'll need to determine how much to let the kid do. A minimal amount of effort here provides a lot of playtime screen-free. How digitized the home no matter or how hooked the kids are to screens, an everlasting fun source is the spinning tops.

6.27 Say Cheese!

It's a time matter only before children tend to understand how everyone needs to capture their images. With this imaginative wooden device, you can create something your talented kid on you will switch right back! No big instruments are needed, but preschoolers can assist with gluing together the pieces and painting them. All you need can be conveniently found across the house or at art shops. One of the toys is this that you would not mind your child playing with for a long time!

6.28 Homemade Stamps

When your kid discovers branches too large for twig creations, it's time to bring a saw, sandpaper, and some little items out there. This is a wonderful art and you can assist your child make wooden stamps of any number. Keep on hand some paint for days like a rainy one and you will have some creative projects always to help your child in making some art in your spare time!

6.29 Friendly Tiny Robot

The nicest thing ever is these wooden DIY robots. It is simple than it appears. Create a treat for a kid or preschooler yourself, or support older kids and high schoolers with basic equipment and blocks of wood. You'll make sufficient for a whole army of robots to take control over the creativity of your child before you know it!

Building this is one of the easiest tasks for kids. Each one is intended to please the younger ones. It's going to be like having a robot pal for your family, one that's large enough to keep the kids happy, and is made up of small enough pieces so that kids get the feel of playing with blocks.

A buddy wooden robot is simple enough to build. You can use your creativity and imagination to create this wooden robot buddy. It's also a concept that makes it possible for the child's imagination to run wild during the creation process.

6.30 DIY Bird Feeder of Wood

This bird feeder in the backyard definitely needs adult supervision. Choose much heavier, thicker, and more durable branches than the tiny twigs from different design ventures, and use for the adhesive, real peanut butter. Perfect is this project for younger and older children alike and parents should help them create this stunning bird feeder.

The older kids should do the task of hammering, while the birdseed and peanut butter should be put up by the little children. So just pick up those binoculars and see all the fun buddies coming in for some snack from your backyard window!

6.31 Little library

Not only can small libraries offer a means for children to learn how to create items, use their thinking, and obey directions, they also understand the importance of interacting with others. You can also register it once you've finished so that anyone can stop to see at the home that what the kids have created.

As you build, you'll want to have in mind the environment, so if you stay anywhere where a lot it rains, you'll want to consider a covered roof for keeping dry everything you want to share.

6.32 Kids' workbench

A perfect place is a workbench to show kids that they often have to create stuff they'd use for daily use. If you're a smart dad, that is exactly the type of stuff that you're going to want the children to select. Besides, it will provide them a chance to feel that they are a bit more grown-up when they start collecting their own toolset.

Like other stuff, this is potentially something you would create using your creative and imaginative skills.

6.33 The bee house

This is good for children who enjoy nature too. Creating a pollinator house provides habitat for bees, and it often makes the children know they are improving the environment of the world. The best thing is these types of bees just occasionally bite, and it's a fairly healthy opportunity for your children to support bees who will keep the garden blooming.

This job isn't that much complex. Moreover, the most difficult device to use in this project is just really a drill. You'll either want to do it yourself or offer much advice to your kids. You'll always want to remember that this thing comes with a canopy to protect the bees from flooding, and you have to design it so that it is as safe from water as possible.

6.34 Wooden planter

This is a very easy project, so if the kids like planting, then it's a perfect start to a summer plan to make a quite small garden. It can be begun by them with some basic plank fastening and end with peppers, radishes, or some basil also.

Much like every other child project, this one can be really personalized based on your designs, or what wanted by you that how the completed planter seems like.

6.35 Birdhouses

Without birdhouses, no collection of DIY projects of woodworking will be sufficient for children. These are good intermediate projects which every child makes up at some time in their childhood. Not only they provide you, friends, with living space but also encourage your children to take more complex actions in dealing with equipment and wood.

6.36 The Folding camp chair

If you're an outdoor person, a tripod chair, folding one is a simple, easy collapsible project that will provide you with a resting place while you're in Outdoors. If used alongside a campfire guitar strumming or by a river tying a harness to some casting rod, the children can love dreaming about their possible adventures while studying how to deal with wood as well as fastening the leather to furniture.

This is not only an easy project to build, but it's also very cheap to put together.

6.37 Camping tent

There's not a lot of woodworking here, practically. It's only fastening few wooden poles together and attaching sheets of fabric alongside a beam that holds them together. However, still, the kids will care if it means a fort can be built by them in a backyard in not more than ten minutes. Would you still want them to learn this can be done by them, and give your kids hours of fun in a really economical way?

You have to give your child a template so he can really stoke his imagination.

6.38 Balance board

For the daredevils inside your family, it's a simple and inexpensive idea. It's a smart way to keep the balance perfect by not having the chance of a chipped tooth or fractured collarbone. Plus, it'll be a lot of fun for the children to create this craft. This needs the usage of the power tools, a bit of fun which might be for children who get frustrated by the comfort and ease of doing things.

Although it seems basic enough for mere creativity activity, you would always want to have the correct wheel proportions so it does not get unbalanced.

6.39 Coat rack of Lego

Although the thought of constructing some coat rack certainly won't excite anybody, it is surely a little more enjoyable to create it out of imaginative Lego designs. It's not complicated to bring together, and it gives parents the extra pleasure of having some game of children cleaning up their spaces.

This actually doesn't look that complex at first glance, but you must consistently use the block bases and circular shapes to achieve the Lego feel and look.

Chapter 7:

Awesome Kids Woodworking Projects with Plans

Few activities are as enjoyable and entertaining, but satisfying as finishing some projects with the children. They have the pleasure of their imaginations using and using devices such as adults, parents enjoy spending time doing something meaningful with the children, which encourages and generates something that the family can be enjoyed for more time.

All of the projects like these are perfect for children. They bring an array of challenges for the kids. This should build a series of tasks so you can switch from the one to next with the increasing difficulty, especially if the children really like to work with their hands. Some of them are very basic and only include wood, glue, and paint. Others demand power tools. This means that they also need a degree of supervision of adults, too. The best thing is the kids will concentrate their imagination at the simplest. Moreover, the kids can also focus their creative skills so that no incorrect responses there are.

In terms of supplies and fasteners, each has its different needs. These also include guidance on how to use the raw materials and images, and the finished product will look like what.

Select the one that is right for your children, and make them enjoy every bit of fun.

7.1 Candy dispenser (Homemade)

Did we mention it can be satisfying to have a woodwork project? Building your candy dispenser is not only a learning experience, but it's something that the kids would love to make because it will give them candy whenever wanted by them.

This includes certain simple hand tools, and parents may have a little more research to do based on age and progress of the motor skills.

Supplies to Build a Candy Dispenser

Given below are the different wooden parts and other materials that you would require to build this candy dispenser:

- 2 inches x 6 inches board, 24 inches long

- 2 1 1/2 inch x 5 1/2 inch x 5 1/2 inch boards for top & base

- 2 1 1/2 inch x 1 3/4 inch x 5 1/2 inch boards for the sides

- 1-inch x 1 7/8 inch x 11 inches board for the slide

- Pencil

- Tape measure

- Pocketknife

- Wood glue

- Sandpaper

- 1 peg or dowel which should be about 1/4 inches in diameter and 4 inches long

- 1 peg or dowel about which should be about1/4 inches in diameter and 2 inches long

- A pint or quart metal ring canning jar

- A crosscut saw that would be used to saw over the grain

- A ripsaw would be required to saw along the grain

- Drill

- Drill bit which would be utilized for the pre-drilling 2 1/2 inches holes

- 7/8 inches spade bit

- Screwdriver

- Countersink bit

- Screws, 12 wood, each 2 1/2 inches long

- 4 brads, flat-head for nailing the jar rings to the dispenser top.

- A tiny drill bit that would be used to pre-drill brad holes in the jar rings

- Gumballs

- Jelly beans

Building a Candy Dispenser

Step-by-step instructions for building a candy dispenser are given below:

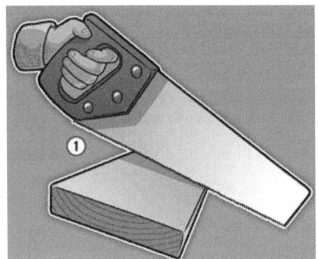
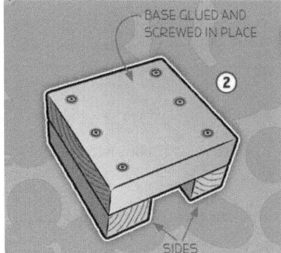

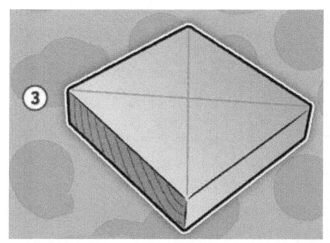

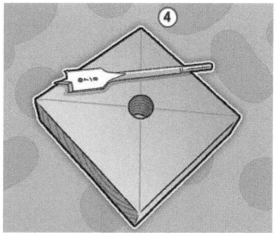

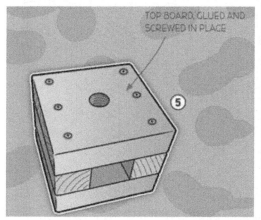

TOP BOARD, GLUED AND
SCREWED IN PLACE

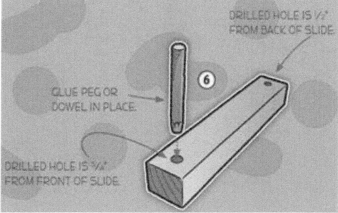

DRILLED HOLE IS ½"
FROM BACK OF SLIDE

GLUE PEG OR
DOWEL IN PLACE

DRILLED HOLE IS ¼"
FROM FRONT OF SLIDE

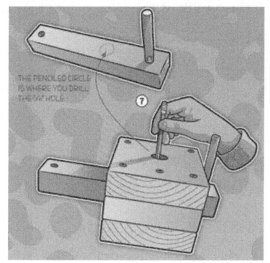

THE PENCILED CIRCLE
IS WHERE YOU DRILL
THE ⅞" HOLE

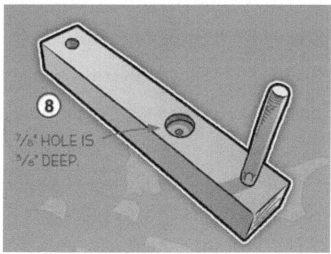

⅞" HOLE IS
⅝" DEEP.

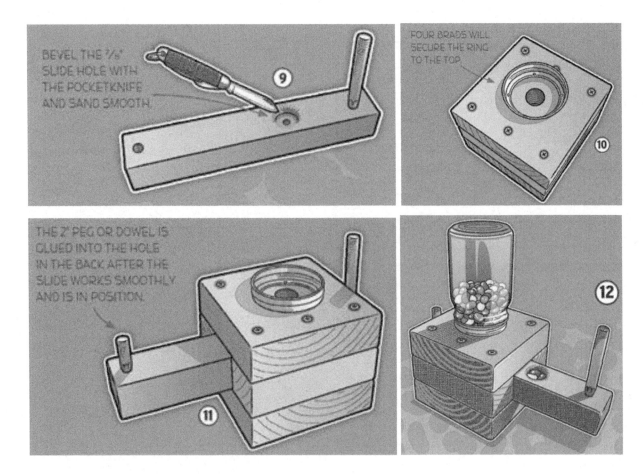

- Cut every board as per specifications and smooth them with sand.

- Then screw and glue base onto sides.

- Draw an X with the pencil from the corner to the corner on top board.

- Drill a 7/8 inches hole through the top board center.

- Screw and glue a top board on the sides and the base. Next, the slide is sand till smoothly it moves in the dispenser center square hole.

- Drill hole of 3/4 inches from the slide, front. This will be used for the 4 inches dowel or peg. Drill hole of 1/2 inches from the slide, back. This will be used for the 2 inches dowel or peg. Glue the 4 inches dowel or peg in the slide front hole.

- The slide is pushed in place till it stops at 4 inches peg. A circle is drawn through the 7/8 inches hole on the slide top board.

- Drill a 7/8 inches hole 3/8 inches deep in the slide.

- Bevel 7/8 inches slide hole by using pocketknife & sand smooth.

- Drill & nail jar rings onto a top board.

- The slide is pushed into the place.

- With candy fill the jar as the dispenser is now complete.

7.2 Catapult

If you always dreamed of learning how to build a catapult, then making this homemade catapult is very easy. Moreover, it is a fun activity for kids of all ages!

Catapult Learning Connections

Listed below are some of the facts concerning catapult:

Engineering

You will learn how to build a catapult that will last long.

Science

It is fantastic for a lecture on physics. The process of pulling back and releasing can teach you about kinetic energy (energy of motion) and potential energy (stored energy). When you pull the cup back you create potential energy. When you expel the energy and start a projectile it is kinetic energy now.

Teach force and velocity. You can change the weight and size of the ball you use to catapult, and test to see if it's going a different height or distance.

History

You should be astonished to know that catapults have been around for a number of years!

How to Build a Catapult?

This is an easy project! Most of the kids could easily make this. Moreover, you do not need to glue guns for this one!

Supplies to Build a Catapult

Given below are the different wooden parts and other materials that you would require to build this catapult:

- 6 wooden dowels - 3 ft. long. These are also easily available at the craft store.

- 9 large rubber bands

- Small plastic cup

- Single-hole punch

- Scissors

- Small balls or any other balls of your choice to launch

Let's begin with building the structure of the catapult. First, make use of three of the wooden dowels. Make them into a triangle by attaching the corners with rubber bands.

Then you pick up another three dowels and attach them as a triangle. However, it must look like a pyramid. You can add one at a time. You should start from each corner of the first triangle. You then connect them using a rubber band.

Now, take the plastic cup and punch three equidistant holes in it.

Break in half three rubber bands, then attach them into the cup's gaps. The other ends of the rubber bands need to be tied to the top of the catapult, and two corners at the bottom. To make this work, you'll need some larger rubber bands. If the rubber bands are not big enough, tie on to the ends on three more runner bands so they can extend the dowels all the way down.

Place a ball in the cup, take it back and let it go! Now you've finished constructing a catapult. Everybody'll be impressed. And you need not tell them how easy it was!

7.3 String Art DIY on Wood

This art gives you the freedom in creating the customized pieces fitting in with your style, personalities, and color scheme. This DIY task can be easily done in less than an hr, and mostly the supplies of the string art are stuff you have, or it can easily get from the near hardware store.

This one for any of the shape templates can work and any string color scheme. You can try a classical white or something like it: it depends on you, really!

It will take at the most about 3 hours, and you and your child will be able to create this in shifts too.

Supplies to Build String Art

Given below are the different wooden parts and other materials that you would require to build this string art:

- Hammer

- Wood

- Many nails

- String

- Masking tape

- Sandpaper

- Template

- Scissors

The wood size always depends on choice, although it is advised that you take a print of the ideal design size before heading towards the woodshop for selecting because you can see the surrounding string art, the negative space. As this creates hideous traces and attracts dust, make sure that masking tape does not leave the adhesive onto the surface.

Building a String Art

Step-by-step instructions for building a string art are given below:

- First, smooth it with sandpaper.

- Take out the Model and print. Around corners be careful. Do not hammer immediately by cutting on the pattern, as there'll be paper pieces and bits sticking onto the nails that will take more time in picking out it than simply scratching out the template.

- After you have fixed the map step back to make sure it's accurate. Masking tape helps hold the diagram in position but reduces the risk of removing stain or the paint off the wood. Make sure you put the nails really close together. If you're having difficulty, tweezers can be used by you to keep the nails in place. When hammering the nails down, the important most thing to keep in mind is that nails must be very much close to one another, allowing only enough room for string to down slipping the middle. Remember to be careful about the accurate hammering of the spikes, down wood going, and along straight lines. More closely spaced the nails the nicer and neater the art of string would be. You may opt to minimize certain sections of the diagram that have so many curves.

- Place the artwork for the personal touch in your home town place! Attempt to the position that in an environment that will create a lot of straight lines as long as possible.

- Use any string color you want, or even combine string colors ... get imaginative with it!

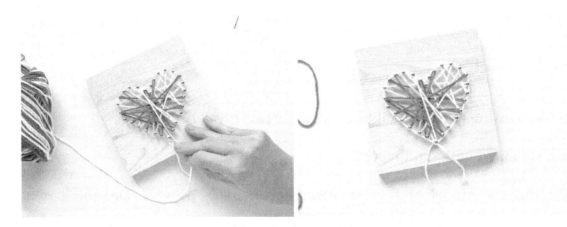

- Loop about the outer side nail, to the heart's nails, bring it, loop it, and to the next state nail, bring it. Just loop once per state nail before continuing onto the next. Nevertheless tend to use the same core nail for the successive loops. This makes between nails, nice tension. To one core tooth, about fifteen state nails there'll be. On the preference of the crafter, this depends. Do not be scared in the string removing and start again until the needed ratio is achieved. Tie the string tail-end to the keys, so it gets fixed properly. This will definitely not be the last idea of string art you're using for creating fun

Chapter 8:

Working Wood Safely With Children and Training Them

People wonder if the woodshop is a very dangerous place for a kid. When a woodshop is such a vulnerable place for a kid, then it is also equally dangerous for any other person irrespective of his/her age. Every child who can write his/her name or inside the lines can color has the dexterity required for securely utilizing most of the hand tools. As a parent, you need to ensure that children comply with the following shop safety principles.

Parents should always devise and then model procedures of safe woodworking

When you don't observe simple safety guidelines yourself then there's no need in guiding everyone. When you want to welcome kids to your shop, you need to observe and at the same practice religiously safety rules and procedures yourself.

Matching the tool and the kid and Vice Versa

There would certainly be eighteen-year-olds you wouldn't trust them with scissors, a lot less a gouge that is used for carving. A kid should be very careful, cautious, meticulous, and watchful of tools enabling you to entrust him/her in sharp tools usage. Know the capacities and limitations of a child. Additionally, make sure that work surfaces and tools are suitable for the child. If some child has to stand on some stool or something like it for reaching a bench-top, be sure that the riser or stool is stable completely and won't slip out of under it. Sometimes, the dangerous most workshop part is the floor. Better yet, it's ideal to make for your kid a bench of kid-sized – about 26 to 28 inches high. Provide hand tools of small-scale, like eggbeater drills of small size, Hammers 8-10 oz., planes # 2 & # 3 for smoothing, and braces 6"-8. And note, a tool with a dull tip is much more harmful than a one sharp.

Demonstrate and Explain techniques of safe handling to kids for every tool

You have to state positively the safety rules: "from yourself, always away cut " instead of "never cut towards yourself;" and "always in a vise or clamp place the workpiece " instead of "never carry a workpiece only with the off-hand of yours." You have to clarify and illustrate each tool cutting force when you show it to your kids. Therefore, they know the meaning of "sharp" is, from both woodworking instruments and kitchen implements. You will not allow dangerous practice in a workshop like horseplay is tolerated. If a kid is too exhausted, too busy, or too upset to function logically, he/she automatically exits the work field.

Supervise Always

Be prepared to put aside your job and watch your kids perform, especially when they're learning to operate an instrument. Stand behind him/her so you're not disrupting the kids. It is because it may be just as harmful to linger in the field of view of the child as not keeping an eye on the kid at all. Let the child focus fully on what he/she is doing. Be Gentle and subtle in fixing incorrect procedure, just don't attempt to snatch a sharp object from the hands of the child as you two can get injured! And whatever you do, ensure just standing back and enjoy. Remember that all of the sharp tools should be locked while you're not around. Your tool chest must be tightly secured, and sharp equipment will then be placed on the mounted wall racks out of the reach of children. Kids grow up, nevertheless. Don't hesitate, to suggest to the kids when they're old enough, to do their job without any supervision.

You should be aware that some of the power tools have the potential to injure people

When children are there, make sure in providing adequate protection for ears, eyes, and breathing systems, if you want to use the power tools — especially table saw, band saw, or driven sander. When your kids are present, you must never use power tools at all as the noise prevents you from to listening what your kids are doing.

You should never expose the children to risk

Be it a 10, 15, or 20 years old person who takes up a sharp instrument for his/her first time, the person can get someone injured. Be frank about the dangers involved in woodworking with the children and also yourself, and assist them to develop in learning early the safe habits of doing work. Your kids need to learn how to use safely the tools as long as they can use them in that manner.

8.1 Safety for Woodworking Kids

Now we are going to share important information that will help keep **kids safe and secure in the workshop.**

Let the Kids take up difficult tasks but under supervision

We need to give some latitude to the kids enabling them to groom and learn how to face intricate and challenging tasks in their future life.

- You need to allow the kids to take things apart. You cannot learn to create and assemble if you do not know how to disassemble and deconstruct.

- Give a jackknife to kids. It is a wonderful tool, and along with other tools the kids will learn and experience amazing things.

- You should not hesitate in letting kids experiment with fire in a safe setting.

Vise Safety Tip

A vise is never one of the tools that we think children might get injured with. A vise is usually more of a safety feature than a hazard. You want to bring children into the practice of holding their piece of work in a vise, rather than trying to hold it by hand. Aside from a piece of work that falls out of the vise, the other possibility is the PINCH that may occur from the vise handle hitting a bit of skin at the end of the handle and the place where the handle sits. The best way to keep a kid's or even an adult's fingers outside of the pinch zone is not to let them get in there. A rubber band wrapped across each end of the vise handle prevents skin from pinching. The rubber bands that perform the best are the fat-blue ones that tie broccoli bunches together. These last forever, and are strong enough to prevent tiny and large fingers from being pinched.

Workshop Ear Safety Tips for Kids

Children's ear protection is just as necessary as it is for workshop adults. In the company of children, you ought to examine carefully the usage of power tools. When attention has been extended to the appropriateness of power tool usage, if the job is noisy, then children require ear protection. That's valid even though they're always banging a hammer at the nails. A few retailers offer ear muffs for kids.

Safety Glasses for Kids

Safety glasses for children should not get fogged up, and should not feel uncomfortable. They have to match to the face of the kid. They should be simpler, more convenient, and the kid should be able and willing to hold them most of the time in the workshop. As they get worse, throw them out and give another to your kid.

It's important that your child has no problem wearing them comfortably. A kid can select his safety glasses and is more likely to select the one which is worn by the parent.

Lead Paint in Tools

If you're using vintage tools for your kids, they may be worth checking out. When you see the lead, or if you see no lead, please mention what you are doing. Test kits are accessible and easily available at most color shops.

Workshop Safety

Many parents are not satisfied with the children being in their shops owing to safety issues. There are special steps that need to be taken while children are around, but don't let this deter you from teaching woodworking to your family, grandchildren, or even the street children. And if you're a parent or grandparent who doesn't have a lot of knowledge about woodworking but your kids are interested, don't let fear, that they'll get hurt, keep you from teaching them.

As adult woodworkers, it is up to us to pass our knowledge down to those who show interest. If we don't, then who is going to? Do not be afraid to allow them in, because they can get injured. A handful of safety tips for parents are given below, while the children accompany them in the workshop.

• Make sure you unplug all of your power tools. You do not need to worry about it once they are unplugged that way.

• Make sure all the blades on your power tools are covered or lowered so that they won't be exposed to small fingers.

• Originally stick to hand tools no matter how old the kids are. Either way, they need that foundation.

• Don't leave your children in the shop unattended, no matter how comfortable you are with their knowledge, maturity, or skill. Accidents will indeed occur.

• Children can wear out quickly using hand tools such as hand-saws. Watch for that, step in at these moments to help out. When children (and adults) get tired, there is a greater chance that errors will occur.

• But, despite the last thing being said; don't do all the children's work only because you can! Let them do the best they should, and be able to encourage them to make their own mistakes. We understand that letting this happen is pretty difficult for the parents.

• Keep things enjoyable for them in the first place! Let them have a say in whatever they build or create. There are so many birdhouses that can be created by a child.

Tools and Materials

It is potentially risky, but woodworking is also satisfying and rewarding at the same time. Tools aren't playthings. The parents ought to supervise the children closely. As parents, you're responsible for the learning of appropriate techniques of woodworking and teaching your children these skills personally. It's a true pleasure to spend time designing with kids, so good judgment should be used and it should be safe.

Children's tools must function properly, without modification. To bring the tools into operation, only a limited amount of expertise will be needed, and they must match tiny hands. Tools present herein are appropriate for up to seven-year-old kids under adult supervision. Stick softer woods such as basswood and white pine. Woods like these are cheap, working easy, and availability is also easy at home.

The kid's Tool kit should contain one each

Given below are the tools that are recommended to be included in the tool kit for kids:

- Safety Glasses – These are imperative for both adults and kids.

- An easy to handle hammer

- Workbench Vise (Portable) – It helps to steadily hold the wood while working on it.

- Coping Saw – This is a perfect tool for children. Moreover, its blades are replaceable and inexpensive, too

- Hand Drill – recommended are the drills of Eggbeater-style as safe to use and fun they are.

- Ten drill bits set 1/16 inches - 1/4 inches (in diameter)

- Pocket Plane – It is quite effective and helps to smooth and shape wood fast. It fits the small hands. Additionally, replaceable is the cutter and doesn't need tuning or sharpening

- Combination Square – For working accurately, you would need a versatile

- 12-ft Tape Measure – It should be strong enough so that if dropped it does not break

- Small Hammer – It should be of a perfect size according to the kid to help him or her in driving nails use

- Wood Glue - set fast this glue of yellow color.

- Rubber Bands – You can as clamps use them when drying glue

- Sandpaper – You should look for grits assorted for surface smoothing. It is also useful for rounding the sharp edges

8.2 It is your Responsibility to Train the Next Generation of Woodworkers

You don't really expect your kids to grow up as professional joiners or carvers — although that would be wonderful — but you want them all to learn how to plane down a sticky fence, fix a cabinet, and push a nail right before they head out alone.

Although your kids may still be very young, you can help them learn a few essential principles to pass on the wood craft to the next generation.

Let them see you work

Shop time is sacred to many of us. It is time we move away from life's anxieties to appreciate the calm phase of creating something special. We admire not just the job we do, but the uncommon solitude as well. Yet if we never open our shops to anyone, both our expertise and wisdom will perish with us and our workshops will just be extensions of our graves.

If we want to pass on our skills – and more, our passion for our craft – we have to invite others to come in, usually one or two at a time. Place the little ones on their tables, stools, or benches from where they can see the hands. You need to be patient with their presence. Let them play in the sawdust. Give them the freedom to explore your shop while you are working. Children gain far more about what we do than what we say.

You must talk as you work

Most woodworkers, and particularly those who gravitate to the hand tools, love the workshop's silence, but if we want to pass on our art, then we will have to be able to crack the silence.

Name the tools you are using when you invite a child in and say what each one is doing for you. Illustrate why you are using one tool instead of another, and clarify how you scrub it before you put it away. The kid won't comprehend everything you're doing, however, he or she can understand better than you can think.

Slow down to make the child pose questions, every so often. You don't have to ask, "No more questions? Kids are willing to watch you work, and would obviously ask questions. Do not be disappointed if there are no questions, but be willing to stop your work for detailed answers to questions. React to queries using small sentences and concise expressions, whenever possible.

Let the Kids putter

Children learn through emulation. Offer a hand tool and some scrap to the boy, and let him or her try it. Small eggbeater drills, belts, spoke shaves, and tack hammers are also suitable tools for really small hands. Children particularly like drawing. They can manage tiny hand planes, carving gouges, and even carving blades, as well as miniature saws, they will be able to do this by the time they are in primary school. Demonstrate the laws of proper use, and state rules as positive rather than negative, whenever possible. "Always cut off from you," for example, instead of "Never cut to yourself."

And don't offer poorly-made tools to children. Even as they frustrate you, they will do nothing but frustrate the child. They are, therefore, more challenging to manage, and therefore more threatening. Let the kids use better tools.

If appropriate, monitor the child use the device and kindly adjust it, but seek to stay behind him or her, and only watch as much as necessary. A cut finger will tell a child more about protection than can a lengthy lesson.

Practice over projects

Children will learn how to use tools just like you learn how to use them. They can accomplish this by practicing on a little scrap until you get the tool feel and understand its capabilities and limitations. Be happy with them covering a board with holes or whittle away a stick to nothing. They don't create projects; they develop skills.

Children will be happy for quite some time by just making chips and shavings. Don't try to force a kid into a project, even if it is a very simple and basic project. You want the child to experience the same comfortable feeling you always find at your store.

When the child has proposed an idea, be prepared to go along with it. You might need to talk a kid down from a very difficult first project or you might need to consider solutions to make it kid-friendly. To tackle this part with a minimum of hassle to help the child create what he or she needs. You should dimension the stock in advance for any first project, and leave only the assembly for the child to do. The satisfaction of seeing a project come together for the child is just as exciting as it is for you.

The relationship is more important than accomplishment

Whether your child ever takes up a tool again in his or her life or not, the child will realize forever that he or she had become a worthy visitor in your sacred space, and that you had taken time to listen and express what had been important to you. Friendship is the most valuable thing you'll ever create in your shop.

If grown are your children?

Of course, there might be grandchildren, nephews, or nieces, or even children from the neighborhood, which can be invited in with permission from their parents. At church or local schools, there might even be children who might be interested in working wood. Keep a close eye for homeschooling children, many of which, as a way of life, are willing to explore arts and crafts. And if you are unable to bring people into your shop, take some of your woodwork to the front lawn. Operating outside is a perfect opportunity to attract visitors into your shop.

It is equally good for grown-ups!

Invite your significant other to hang around for a while, while you operate. This could be possible only if you are in a partnership. You'll learn as much about a person, especially a man, by watching him function as you speak to him about it. So your significant other shall develop a deeper respect for the job that you do. Kids are your main project, and you spend your lifetime on finishing this wonderful project, but it is never finished

This isn't easy

If you let your child move into your shop, then it is not all rainbows and roses. You may not find it pleasing to communicate with your child by pausing on a project in the shop, particularly while you are operating on a tight deadline. When your kids reorganize the trays in your tool chest you have to suppress your annoyance, and when they break you're sharpening stones or use your machinist's square as a mallet, you have to contain your fury. Yet such interruptions will never be regretted. Repairing a broken tool is easier than fixing a broken relationship.

Kid-Friendly Woodworking Projects

Given below are some beautiful crafts that with your kids you can try and make.

Tool chest

It is assembled usually with nailed rabbets. This leads to simple joinery, and quick is the assembly. It provides kids a maneuvering room to put to test their knowledge of tools.

Doll furniture

This one's for the girls particularly. Small stools and tables are extremely popular with children. But don't get a picture of delicate moldings and tiny cabriole legs of elegant furniture.

Angled holes bore in a wood piece and dowels glue/wedge for legs. Then the girls will color and try out their art. If it's a large piece, doll table it is; it's a doll chair if it's a little piece.

Stools of Regular-sized

These are simple to sit on, particularly triple-legged stools. Your kids should switch the brace for drilling and holes reaming and handle the cutter tapered tenon which suits them. If a circular seat is cut out by you in advance, this is a close-perfect project for kids.

Nailed boxes

These are fairly easy, too. The rabbets nailed hold well together and usually, they can be made with off-cuts. Cutting nails requires a pilot hole that is fun as both a hammer and eggbeater drill are used by the children.

Seek to scale the project pieces ahead of the time, if you may. The child and you on the enjoyable parts can focus such as assembly and joinery. There'll come a period where you decide to send an older child through the entire cycle of the stock selection, doing dimensioning, doing joinery, doing assembling, and then finishing, and with their persistence and perseverance, certain young children will delight you. Set realistic expectations for the attention time of a child, but do not discount a committed child's attention span.

Anything the kids put up in the shop with you, inspire the kids to stay until the end of the project. Moreover, don't hesitate in smiling and joking during this. Ultimately what you create doesn't mean as much as the quality time spent by you and your kid. artwork.

Conclusion

Playing with tools provides one of the strongest skills to youth, which lets youth get organized and motivated about the dreams of their potential lives. For children, the desire to make something is so universal that they are able to go through a lot of hard work to accomplish their goals. It is more of a discipline. Kids must go to the woodshop to attain the following:

• Exercise and emphasize perseverance

• Build subtle and gross motor expertise, and integrate hand-eye movement

• Develop socially and emotionally through self-assurance, accountability, self-esteem, and appreciation for supplies and protection

• The tradition of communicating and living together

• Explore abstract reasoning (size, form, distance, geometry, and dimensionality), skills in engineering, and creativity;

Kids learn a range of woodworking techniques as well as various methods of playing specific instruments. However, some of the shop's more extensive instruction is linked to character growth. Woodworking lets children concentrate their attention on:

• Creating self-esteem such that children finish the phrase "I can't do that" on a daily basis with the term "yet."

• Production of the emotional endurance and analytical ability required to overcome challenges and benefit from errors.

• Take moral accountability for your own job and for the personal health and welfare of everyone around you.

• Recognizing the true work-related satisfaction is achieved through achieving targets you set yourself or truly accepted as yourself.

As a woodshop is stocked with kid-sized tools, so the children are the only ones strong enough to do the right work. Tools are also even useful for the growth of children's bodies, strength, stamina, and skills. Children who have shown enough skill and concentration to use them safely can even be given power tools. The lathe can be your most popular tool for making stunning lamps and bowls with the kids.

The "tinker desk" is a spot where students will deconstruct outdated electrical gadgets and home appliances and see how they function, or to find out how to repair them. Children may begin to learn the fundamentals of electronics and incorporate disassembled computer parts into their woodworking ventures. Children will be able to create their own ideas, given they will complete a project before beginning another.

This teaches them commitment, and how to persevere with something when they are bored or tired.

As kids grow up and develop their abilities, they are progressively trying ambitious projects. You will help kids create go-carts, tables, benches, and even a chicken coop.

In a day and age where boys are disproportionately involved throughout group events such as clubs and competitive sports and absorbed in the internet and video games, it may be challenging for busy parents to create intimate interactions with their sons. If you're looking for a fun, educational, and valuable activity to do with your child, father and son woodworking projects are an exceptional way to get there. Knowing how to use your hands and minds to create things offers children a feeling of faith and success whilst giving them a full range of abilities that they will apply in their life in several different ways.

One thing that's great for kids about woodworking is that you can start out at a very young age. Although every infant grows differently, several tasks are suitable for fathers and sons from the ages of five or six and up. Getting used to using the tools and performing simple tasks like early drilling and sawing helps build a lifelong hobby which feels like second nature.

Best Father and Son Woodworking Projects

Choosing the right woodworking projects for father and son is relatively straightforward. Firstly, you'll want to acknowledge the age, period of interest, and motor abilities of your infant, as well as your degree of experience. Do not hesitate if you are not a professional craftsperson or a carpenter. There are almost endless projects to choose from which beginners can accomplish, and as you learn together it will be even more of a bonding experience.

Perhaps the smartest way to choose woodworking projects for your father and son is by focusing on what your children are interested in or would find meaningful. Creating the first "big kid" bed or work station, dolls, or a crate to store them in and a backyard park bench or tree house are some of the popular ventures. Even something as simple as a puzzle game or pirate sword can be a pleasant introduction that will help your son get to know the tools, vocabulary, and woodworking skills.

Sharing Woodworking Joys

When you do woodworking projects with your son, it is necessary to note that it's more about the method than the outcome. While you are able to produce something that can be shared together and eventually become a family heirloom, the real value is in the lessons experienced and the time invested improving consistency together.

Sharing common moments is one of the strongest ways to create good memories. Woodworking should be used in this way to build the connections that last. Did you get a handy kid? You certainly do! You know the little ones will impress you with what they will achieve if you give them the opportunity to teach you, that is. At the thought of your kid using a hammer or a saw in those small hands, you shouldn't be cringed.

There are plenty of woodworking projects your little guys may do. You can teach them to use tools properly and the things they can do with them will definitely amaze you. To keep your kids inspired and creating, you should and need to find some woodworking projects for kids.

In fact, woodworking is very easy to learn from the onset. You'll most definitely want your kid to create things and that's what he'll learn about. Woodworking is a method of continuous learning because it is only one project at a time. Training that way will hold your child focused. Never stress him with too much more than he can cope with at one time.

. . . .

Thank you for buying this book.

Made in the USA
Las Vegas, NV
20 November 2020